Flavors

OF

St. Augustine

An Historic Cookbook

By

Maggi Smith Hall

Illustrations by

Jean Light Willis

Dedication

*This book is dedicated to
the generations of cooks
who proceeded us
and to
those who will follow.*

For information about permission to reproduce selections from this book, write to Permissions, Tailored Tours Publications, Inc., Box 22861, Lake Buena Vista, Florida 32830.

Printed in the United States of America.

ISBN: 1-892629-01-1

Cover design by Mark Kellum, Success by Design
Book design by Nina McGuire, Tailored Tours Publications, Inc.
Illustrations by Jean Light Willis, Jean Light Willis Studio

Table of Contents

*T*able of *C*ontents, *continued*

Table of Contents, continued

Acknowledgements

*W*ithout the perceptive talent of our editor and publisher, Nina McGuire, who saw through a rough draft to the possibilities beyond, there would be no book. Nina, we thank you.

Our appreciation extends to the owners, directors, and staffs of the historical properties who lent their expertise to our project: the late Page L. Edwards, Jr., Executive Director of the St. Augustine Historical Society; David Nolan, St. Augustine Historian; Eddie Joyce Geyer, Acting Director of the St. Augustine Historical Society; Taryn Rodriguez-Boette, Library Director, and Charles A. Tingley, Research Librarian, at the St. Augustine Historical Society Research Library; Nella Holton at Government House; Kathy Fleming, Director, and Sue Van Vleet, Assistant Director of the St. Augustine Lighthouse Museum Complex; Robert W. Harper, III, Director, and Barry Myers, Lightner Museum; James Craig Morris, Brad Shattuck, and Greg Utech, Park Rangers, Fort Caroline National Memorial of the Timucuan Ecological and Historic Preserve; Dana Ste.Clare, Curator of History, Science, and Archaeology, The Museum of Arts and Sciences; Guy Tillis, Director of the Ximenez-Fatio House; the Fraser Family of the Oldest Wooden Schoolhouse and the Fountain of Youth; Fran Powell of The Woman's Exchange; the Florida Society of Colonial Dames of America; and Carl Miller at the Oldest Store.

We applaud the efforts of those who tested our recipes and proofed our manuscript: Margie and Chip Beacher, Cherry Hall, Suzanne Beasley, Chef James A. Pelli, III of Flagler College, Jeanette Mackin, Kat Twine, Rachel Daniels Lightsey, Wilma Daniels Thompson, Cathy Brown, Taylor Scott, Ron Hall, and members of the Andreu, Smith, Latimer, and Lehman Families.

Gratitude is given to those who assisted in numerous other ways: Ellen Begovich, Christine Barrett, Cory and Tommy Gillilland, Nancy Garrard, Gudrun Baroth, Janie Young Price, Joe Taylor, Bob Talton, Karen Harvey, Jason Stout, and Susan Grohmann. And to our Spanish translators, Sara Fasey and Isobel and Francisco Romanach, a hearty "muchas gracias."

To the owners and chefs of the inns and restaurants who generously shared their recipes, we graciously offer thank you: Bill and Diane Johnson of Carriage Way Bed and Breakfast, Bob and Donna Marriott of Casa de La Paz, Bruce and Kimmy VanKooten Kloeckner of Castle Garden, Joe Finnegan and Chef Terry Jackson of the St. Francis Inn, Russ and Nina Thomas of the Cedar House Inn, Nancy Noloboff of the Secret Garden Inn, the Ponce Family of the Conch House Marina Resort, Len and Kristy Weeks of the Florida Cracker and La Parisienne, Lori Hollar of the Café Alcazar for recipes created by Maureen Crescenzo; and Darcy and Chef John Compton of the Casa Monica Hotel Restaurant.

We also wish to recognize the work of the book production team of Jenny Caneen, Michele Caneen, Mark Kellum, Sara Lee, Don Schroeder, and Mary Theuret.

Lastly, we especially acknowledge our families who provided us the ingredients of love, patience, and encouragement needed to complete this project. Jean particularly thanks Nancy and Sam Ehling and the entire Willis Clan. I am grateful to my supportive husband, Ron, and our daughters and their families: Erin and Justin Holder and Amy, Roger, Zac, Nash, and Gabe Dendinger.

Publisher's Note

*W*e wish to briefly comment on a few decisions made concerning historical usage. For years, early northeastern Florida Native Americans were known as Timucuan. However, current research confirms their name as Timucua, with Timucuan being the adjective. In the late 1700s, the Spanish governor's family name was de Zéspedes. In later generations, the spelling became Céspedes. Several wonderful, colorful fables, legends, and folk tales have grown up in St. Augustine and a few of them are included in the book. Most notably is the story of Ponce de León's landing in the St. Augustine area. Research in the 1990s strongly suggests that he landed at least 60 miles south, perhaps within 8 nautical miles of Melbourne Beach, and yet, in St. Augustine, a delightful, romantic legend persists.

*I*ntroduction

*F*ive *F*lags and a *T*housand *F*lavors

*S*t. Augustine captivates its visitors! Tourists return again and again to walk its narrow streets, to visit its historical sites, and to marvel at its natural beauty and old world charm. Its landscape is diverse. From ancient coquina buildings to the playful tug of ocean waves, St. Augustine offers a variety of unique features.

St. Augustine captivates its residents! As a permanent settlement, it dates back over 400 years, making it the oldest continually occupied city in the United States. Its culture is diverse. From its earliest inhabitants to the present, St. Augustinians have a variety of unique stories to tell.

Flavors of St. Augustine captures this diversity and charm. Several years of research and sketching have been blended to present the long-ago accomplishments and tastes of those who hunted our forests, cultivated our soil, and fished our waterways.

The book tells of determined people who loved our town and built its lasting traditions. It contains historical menus and gives recipes, some of which have been derived from food remains excavated at archaeological sites. And it offers authentic dishes which reflect the foods available to St. Augustine's inhabitants throughout its history.

Today's cook can step back into the city's past by experimenting with its recipes and reading its stories. A few recipes may seem bland or extra spicy; others unfamiliar to our modern palate. But most are truly delicious.

Flavors of St. Augustine tells the story of our town by presenting the history of its inhabitants through their eating habits, recipes, and cooking and preservation techniques. We invite you to bring our city's fascinating heritage into your home through a "cook's tour" of captivating St. Augustine—the city of five flags and a thousand flavors.

Maggi Smith Hall
Bay Breeze Cottage
St. Augustine, Florida

Chapter I.
The Timucua
Pre–1565

The earliest migration of Native Americans into present-day Florida took place over 15,000 years ago. Their diet consisted of wild game and wild plants. Few changes occurred in their culture until sometime around 5000 BC when they added mollusks and fish, snails and shellfish to their diets. When they cooked their food it was over an open fire pit. In 2000 BC their cooking methods expanded with the creation of clay pots and the heating of flat stones for baking. By the time the first Europeans set foot on Florida's soil in the early 1500s AD, the Timucuan Indians of Northeast Florida had evolved from nomadic hunters and gatherers to skilled farmers, cultivating maize, squash, pumpkin, and beans.

The remains of Timucuan shell middens along the waterways of Northeast Florida indicate that the Timucua liberally ate salt and freshwater mollusks. These middens included not only oyster and clam shells, but animal bones, pottery sherds, and broken projectile points. As the centuries passed these piles of cultural materials grew in breadth and height. Sixteenth century sailing records document the visibility of the Timucuan shell mounds from a distance of three miles at sea. Many middens remain today, but are difficult to see due to coverage by soil and silt. During the Spanish occupation of Northeast Florida material from the mounds was used to build and then later repair coquina structures. Recycling shells from middens continued through the mid–20th century for use in road construction.

What does remain of these middens has allowed modern man to understand better the Timucua culture and their eating habits. Their well-balanced diet no doubt contributed to their longevity and to their physical stature; both men and women were often six feet tall.

The Timucua were noted for their ornately tattooed bodies created by rubbing soot or berry juice into self-inflicted wounds.

When the Spanish arrived in Florida, they were greeted warmly by these imposing Indians. The explorers recorded their observations of the Timucua, their social structure, their religious beliefs, and their food preparation. They wrote of how the Indians smoked meat on wooden sticks or roasted game in a little house set on a raised platform above an open fire. The Spanish described their technique as "barbacoa" from which we derive the word "barbecue."

Archaeological excavations and Spanish records indicate that the Timucua also enjoyed coontie palm, prickly pears, wild onions, persimmons, muscadine grapes, hog and coco plums, honeycombs, and honey. Besides seafood, they also ate venison, rabbit, raccoon, opossum, beaver, bear, gopher and sea turtles and their eggs, alligator, rattlesnake, and birds.

Little is known about the spices they ate. We do know, however, that the Timucua used salt to preserve fish. This fact probably indicates that they also added salt to their meals. Salt, of course, was obtained by evaporating ocean water. Records show that they made extracts from fermented fruits, berries, barks, and roots. Since the bay leaf grew in abundance in Northeast Florida, we think it is likely that they tested its rich flavor.

Originally, the Indians used sticks and stone blades for cooking utensils, later advancing to carved wooden spoons and clay pottery.

Early on, they used their fingers for eating. As their cooking became more advanced, they created knives by polishing bone. The Timucua drank from gourds and shell cups.

Food was protected in woven baskets, clay pots, or wrapped in animal skins. In order to preserve foods they salted and smoked fish and sun-dried fruits.

Several of the plants and animals which the Timucua ate are now on federal endangered, threatened, or commercially exploited lists, so be prepared to make substitutions as noted in the recipes.

The Hunter

Roasted Bear

The Florida Black Bear is on the federal threatened species list. If you have any friends who hunt for bear elsewhere in the United States and who might have a freezerful of bear roasts, trade them dinner for the meat. Assuming you locate this wild game, build an open fire pit away from flammable material and begin cooking when the coals are hot and glowing.

3–5 lbs bear roast

Wash and clean the bear roast thoroughly. Skewer the meat and rotate it over an open fire pit for 8–10 hours. Yields 6–10 servings.

Barbecued Opossum

Opossum should be cleaned as soon after hunting as possible. Hang meat for 48 hours before skinning and cooking. Remove the excess fat to avoid strong taste and odor.

1 opossum roast, sliced

Skewer opossum on spit. Barbecue it over the open fire 4–6 hours until cooked through and brown. Yields 6–8 servings.

Anastasia Dune Rabbit

3 rabbits, cleaned, disjointed
2 c squash, quartered
2 c pumpkin, diced
1/2 c sea grape juice (or lemon juice)
1/2 c fat
1 c water
4 bay leaves, whole (the Timucua used
    leaves from the Carolina Bay trees
    which grew along the coast)
1/2 t salt

In a large pot, brown the rabbits in fat. Add water, juice, and bay leaves. Bring to a boil and simmer, covered, 1–1/2 hours or until meat is tender. Remove meat from the pot and debone. Place the meat back into the pot and add vegetables. Simmer for 20 minutes or until the vegetables are done. Yields 6 servings.

Fried Raccoon

1 raccoon, cleaned, sliced
24 c water
1/2 c water
10 bay leaves
3/4 c water

1/2 c fat
1 c Florida coontie palm root, grated
    (Although the Timucua would have
    used a coontie palm root for flavoring
    and as a starch source, today both the
    Florida coontie and east coast coontie
    are on the federal commercially ex-
    ploited list. Today's cook should substi-
    tute with 1 c cornmeal.)

Place the raccoon in a large pot and soak it overnight in water and bay leaves. The following day, parboil in the same water for 20 minutes. Drain and wipe the meat dry. Combine 1/2 cup water and palm root to make a smooth batter. Dip the raccoon slices in the batter and drop it into hot fat. Brown on all sides. Add remaining water, reduce heat, cover, and cook slowly until tender, approximately 2 hours. Yields 6–8 servings.

Char–Spit Venison

1 venison loin cut in half, pierced deeply
    every inch

Marinade:
4 T coco plums (from the coconut palm),
    crushed
6 bay leaves, crushed
1 c palm berries, mashed
1 c lard
1 c corn drink (or whiskey)
1 c water

Marinate loin overnight. The following day, remove loin from marinade and skew on a spit. Save marinade to use for basting. Cook meat over hot coals, basting and turning every 15 minutes for 2 hours or until tender. Yields 6–8 servings.

Roasted
White–tail Deer

2 lbs deer steaks, cut into serving pieces
3 T lard
2 bay leaves, crushed
1 c wild berries, crushed (juniper
    berries from the Red Cedar tree)
1 c corn drink (or whiskey)
1 c Florida coontie palm root, grated
    (today's cook should substitute with
    1 c ground cornmeal)
1 c beans, cooked, mashed
1 t salt

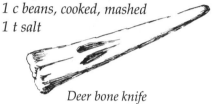

Deer bone knife

Moisten meat and dredge in palm root. Brown in hot lard. Mix remaining ingredients and pour over steak. Let sit for several hours. Remove meat from liquid and skewer on individual sticks. Hold over flame and roast until cooked through. Yields 4–6 servings.

White-tail Deer and Squash Stew

The Florida fig ripens in August and is a favorite of people, blue jays, and mockingbirds. Wild onion can be eaten from spring through fall. If you dig up its root, leave part of the root in the ground for next year's crop.

3–1/2 lbs deer, cubed
4 figs, mashed
2 lbs squash, thickly sliced
4 bay leaves
6 c water
1 c wild onions (or commercial onions),
    sliced
1 t salt

Place venison, water, figs, salt, onions, and bay leaves in a pot and simmer uncovered for 2 hours or until meat is tender. Add squash and simmer, covered, 15 minutes. Yields 6–8 servings.

The St. Johns River is one of the few rivers in the world to flow north. The Timucua would have called the river "Ibi ainan(ta)," which means "its way is contrary to all others." The St. Johns travels north for hundreds of miles, ultimately emptying into the Atlantic Ocean at Mayport, Florida. Also named the River of May by French explorer Jean Ribault in May, 1562, it was Florida's first "major" highway. Its dark winding trail is home to various wild and edible creatures as well as the chalky substance out of which the Timucua molded their pottery.

St. Johns River Beaver

1 beaver, cleaned
1 c coco plum, crushed
1/2 c fat
3 c water
6 bay leaves, crumbled
1 c pumpkin seeds, crushed

Combine all ingredients then rub the beaver inside and out with the mixture. Place on a spit over hot coals, turn slowly, and roast 5–7 hours, depending on the size of the beaver. Yields 8–10 servings.

The Timucua captured alligators by camouflaging a brave hunter in a 'gator skin, head and tail included. The hunter would then crawl toward a 'gator den and give a few deep growls. Usually a curious 'gator would answer the call by lunging from its nest where waiting hunters would thrust a long thin debranched tree trunk into its open jaws.

The most tender and delicious part of the 'gator is its tail. Although the Florida alligator was once endangered, it is now hunted during open season. The State of Florida also allows a portion of the alligator eggs to be transferred from their nests to an alligator farm where they are hatched. The 'gators are then raised and later sold for meat and other by-products. 'Gators that prove a danger or a nuisance are harvested by state-licensed alligator trappers.

If watching 'gators is more your style than hunting or eating them, visit the St. Augustine Alligator Farm, one of Florida's first tourist attractions. It opened in 1893 along the banks of Salt Run on Anastasia Island and relocated to its present site on A1A in 1937.

Alligator Tail

2 lbs alligator tail, thinly sliced
1 c cornmeal
1/4 c fat
4 bay leaves, shredded
1 t salt

Dredge 'gator in meal and bay leaves. Heat fat in pot and fry meat until golden brown. Drain. Serves 4–6.

In 1513 Spanish explorer Juan Ponce de León, said to be in search of the elusive Fountain of Youth, landed along the east coast of Florida, perhaps as far north as Melbourne Beach or Ponce de León Inlet. Because it was spring and the fragrance of blossoms overwhelming, Ponce de León named this new land La Pasqua de Florida for its "parade of flowers." He then continued south and west along the coast.

A devout Catholic, he marked in sand the location of his landing. Using ballast from his ship, he placed 15 stones in the ground laid east to west. Those stones were crossed by 13 stones laid north to south creating a religious symbol to depict the year of de León's discovery.

When all of the stones were in place, Ponce de León proclaimed:

> Thanks be to Thee, O Lord, Who hast permitted me to see something new.
>
> Ponce de León, 1513

Over the next few decades, the Spanish continued to explore this new paradise. The French also became interested in La Florida because of its proximity to the trade route from Central and South America. In 1562 the French naval captain Jean Ribault was sent to scout the territory. Sailing along the coast, near pres-

Stone Cross

ent day St. Augustine Inlet, Ribault was so impressed by the dolphins at play in the bay that he named it the River of Dolphins. Soon after, Ribault, and several hundred men, women, and children sailed north to the mouth of the St. Johns River where they built Fort Caroline.

> *. . . [W]e entered in to a goodly and great river, which as we went we found to increase still in depth and lardgness, boylling and roring through the multytute of all sortes of fishes . . . . They [Natives] presented us with . . . ffishe, as crabbes, lopsters, crevices [crawfish] and many other kindes of good ffishes.*
>
> Jean Ribault, 1562

Florida Wild Turkey Stuffed with Sea Grapes and Nuts

3 lbs turkey, dressed
1 c sea grapes, seedless, crushed
18 juniper berries, dried, crushed
1 c pine nuts, chopped
1/4 c corn drink (or whiskey)
palmetto leaves (or aluminum foil)
1 t salt

Rub bird inside and out with salt. Mix grapes, berries, nuts, and corn drink. Stuff turkey with the mixture, then skewer opening shut and truss. Wrap remaining stuffing in well washed palmetto leaves (or aluminum foil). Place bird on a spit over an open fire or barbecue house and roast 2-3 hours. The wrapped stuffing can be placed near hot coals for cooking. Yields 6-8 servings.

The Gatherer

From crevices and crabbes, lopsters and ffishes, berries and plants, the Timucua gathered a wide variety of foods for their families, generously sharing their provisions with the pale strangers who visited their abundant land.

Boiled Crevices

Crawfish are caught in shallow brackish water. To attract their attention, toss pieces of old meat or chicken necks into the water near shore and wait with patience and a long–handled net.

2 lbs crawfish
1 c bay leaves, whole
10 c water
2 T coco plum, crushed
4 ears corn
2 t salt

Place all spices in water and bring to a boil. Boil 10 minutes. Add crawfish and corn. When water returns to a boil, cook 10 minutes. Remove from heat and allow to sit for 5 additional minutes to add flavor. Yields 4 servings.

Archaeologists excavating a prehistoric Indian site along the North River near Vilano Beach, about eight miles from St. Augustine, discovered that both the Stout Tagelus and Coquina were highly prized by the Timucua. The Stout Tagelus, a member of the Sanquin Clam family, is noted for its rich flavor. Found in shallow sand banks between tide marks, it lives in a vertical position in the sand and feeds with part of its shell sticking out, thus facilitating gathering. The Coquina or Donax, equally delicious, lives in warm water close to shore. It shows great variation in color and markings and is easily identified by its pastel shades and butterfly wings.

Both the Tagelus and the Coquina can be gathered in late summer along the coast in northeast Florida as ocean waves sweep back the granules of sand. But be prepared with scoop and sieve as these fast–digging creatures disappear within seconds of discovery.

Tagelus or Coquina Broth

8 c Tagelus or Coquina
water to cover
3 bay leaves, whole
1 c coconut milk (or cream and butter)
1 t salt

Hold mollusks in a sieve under running water until thoroughly separated from sand particles. Place in pot and barely cover with water. Add bay leaves and bring to a boil, then reduce heat and simmer until the shells pop open. Remove from heat and drain liquid into a clean pot. Discard the shells. Add salt. Enrich with coconut milk or cream and butter. Yields 4–6 servings.

Jacques Le Moyne, a renowned French artist, was part of an expedition in 1564 and was one of the few people to escape the Spanish massacre of 1565. On returning to France, LeMoyne produced 42 drawings of scenes from that trip.

> To keep their food a little longer . . . they set four forked stakes in the ground and placed other wooden sticks on top. On this frame the Indians lay the animals and fish, with a fire underneath to cure them with the smoke. They take great care to smoke the meat thoroughly so it would not spoil.
>
> Jacques Le Moyne de Morgues, 1564

Grilled Smoked Mullet

2 mullet, halved
2 bay leaves, crushed
2 T fat
1/4 c corn drink (or whisky)
1/2 c bananas, cooked, mashed
banana leaves (or aluminum foil)

Place fish on banana leaves. Combine remaining ingredients and spread over fish. Fold leaves, making sure there is no leakage. Place on wooden frame (or grill) over hot coals. Turn once every 20 minutes being careful not to tear wrapping. Smoke 2-3 hours. Remove fish from wrapping and save sauce. Place fish directly on frame for 5 minutes. Turn fish once and leave for another 5 minutes, occasionally basting with sauce. Yields 4 servings.

Charcoal Shrimp and Squash

24 lg shrimp, peeled
4 squash, cut in large chunks
1/2 c honey

Alternate shrimp and squash on skewer. Place on wooden frame (grill) over hot coals and grill about 2 minutes on one side. Flip the skewer and cook until shrimp turn pink. Squash will be crunchy. Baste with honey. Yields 2 servings.

Although Juan Ponce de León never located the fabled spring of eternal youth, the Timucua had access to healthy water supplies. Their choices included water from pure flowing artesian springs and natural sulfur wells, the latter still treasured by many in the region. Beware, to those not familiar with sulfur water, it smells like rotten eggs and tastes very much the same. To reduce its odor, let it sit overnight so the putrid gas will dissipate.

My authorities unanimously declare that they have heard of the fountain which restores vigor . . . . They have a Bahamian servant . . . born of a very aged father, who from his native land near the region of Florida, attracted by the fame of that fountain . . . left to take the longed–for waters . . . . He . . . spent some time there, bathing in and drinking the water . . . and . . . returned home with virile efficacy, acquitted himself in his masculine duties, and . . . married again and had children. This son presents as proof of it . . . .
Peter Martyr d'Anghiera, 1516

The stone cross which Ponce de León laid in the sand in 1513 may have been discovered in the 20th century, perhaps near Jupiter, Palm Beach, or on Pine Island on the west coast. However, long before that significant discovery, the tourist attraction, The Fountain of Youth, had opened. Visitors to this popular spot are offered a sip from its natural free-flowing spring. If you're wondering whether that spring could be the elusive waters of eternal hope, there's only one way to find out.

Artifacts unearthed at the Fountain of Youth also revealed it to be the site of the Timucua village of Seloy. Interestingly enough, the Spanish recorded that the Timucua were noted for their vigorous health, height, and longevity. Perhaps it wasn't the fresh spring water that made them so notably robust. Perhaps it was something stronger that they drank.

Although water and the corn drink were the most commonly consumed beverages of the Timucua, their more potent drinks were made from berries, roots, bark, twigs, and leaves, gathered and then boiled in water until the liquid became stained with tannin. It was a matter of ritual that the Timucua men met formally to make decisions that affected their tribe. During these council sessions they took turns imbibing in their ceremonial "Black Drink" served in a conch shell.

This caffeine–rich drink was brewed from the dried leaves of the native Yaupon Ilex vomitoria Aiton, a thick evergreen native to the maritime forests of Florida. To Native Americans the Black Drink had the power to purge evil spirits from the body, thus allowing visions of past and future events to enlighten tribal leaders.

Black Drink

1 c Yaupon leaves, dried
4 c water
1 c honey

Combine leaves and water in a pot. Bring to a boil and then remove from heat. Allow the mixture to steep for 2 hours. Add honey for a more palatable brew. Yields 4 servings.

Honey Tea

2/3 c honey
4 c water

Place honey and water in an airtight container. Blend by shaking well. Yields 4 servings.

The Maypop or Passion Flower as it is more commonly called, derives its name from the "popping" sound the fruit makes when mashed. It grows wild along roadsides, but is also cultivated for its attractive ornamental trailing vine and lavender blossoms.

Maypop Juice

4 c maypops
4 c water
1/2 c honey

Use only ripe maypop fruits which are yellow in color and somewhat shriveled. Place fruit in pot and add water. Simmer 30 minutes. Strain fruit through a cloth then return to the pot. Add honey and stir well. Yields 4 servings.

The Farmer

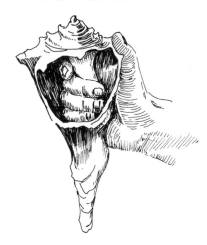

Farming tools were crafted from the Florida whelk, the conch, or stone which they bartered from Indians dwelling to the north and west.

Unlike their neighbors to the south, the Tequesta Indians, the Timucua became adept at agriculture.

Estimates of the Timucuan population when the Europeans settled the continent numbered beyond 25,000. And despite the fact that between 1513 and 1565 their peaceful life was interrupted by foreign explorers, the Timucua managed to endure.

Good fortune eluded the Spanish conquistadors, as their exploration of La Florida was clouded by one disappointment after another. As an example, in 1528, Pánfilo de Narváez began an exploration for gold and silver. *Accompanying him were a band of soldiers, including Cabeza de Vaca, and priests, whose mission was to save the souls of the Indians.*

Governor Narváez ordered that the brigantine should sail along the coast of Florida and search for the harbor. After the brigantine left, the same party . . . returned to enter the land. We kept along the shores of the bay . . . and, having gone four leagues, we captured four Indians. We showed them maize, to see if they had knowledge of it . . . . They said they could take us where there was some; so they brought us to their town near by, at the head of the bay, and showed us a little corn not yet fit for gathering.

Cabeza de Vaca, 1542

After the expedition abandoned its ship to march inland in search of food, the explorers became hopelessly lost, wandering for days. Finally, as a last resort, they killed their horses for food. Eventually reaching the Gulf of Mexico, the survivors built makeshift boats hoping to float to Cuba; but many died in the surf. The remaining few soldiers and priests headed west on foot. Seven years later, only four men from the Narváez expedition reached the Pacific Ocean, among them de Vaca. Other adventurers followed, including Hernando de Soto, but all ultimately failed in their attempt to gain riches.

Meanwhile, the Timucua continued farming their land, fishing their waters, and living their lives—for a while longer at least.

Indian Corn Pudding

3 c corn
1/2 c fat
1/2 c water
2 T cornmeal
1/4 c corn drink (or whiskey)
1/4 c honey
1 t salt

Combine all ingredients in shallow pot. Cook on a wooden frame (or grill) over hot coals for 20-30 minutes or until mixture is solid. Check frequently so as not to burn. Yields 4 servings.

The Timucua used bowls made of stone to grind corn.

Baked Squash

4 squash, quartered
4 T pumpkin seeds, crushed
2 bay leaves, crumbled
2 T fat
1 c wild onion, sliced (or commercial onion)
1 t salt

Place a layer of squash and onion in the bottom of a dish and dot with half of the fat.

An Indian bowl of this type
was used between 500 BC and 1700 AD.

Mix seasonings and sprinkle half over the layer of squash. Add a second layer of squash and onion and repeat process. Cook on a wooden frame (or grill) over hot coals for 30 minutes. Stir squash lightly once, pushing the top layers to the bottom and lifting the bottom layer of squash to the top. Continue cooking until done. Watch carefully as may burn. Yields 4 servings.

Timucuan Bean Balls

2 c beans
4 c cornmeal
3 c water
1 t salt

Boil beans in water over hot coals until tender. Remove beans from water and place in meal and salt with enough bean juice to form a stiff dough. Roll mixture into balls then drop carefully back into the pot of boiling bean juice. Cook 20-30 minutes at a slow boil. Yields 4–6 servings.

Grilled Pumpkin

1 sm pumpkin
2 T honey
2 T fat
1/4 c corn drink (or whiskey)

Wash the pumpkin well and place on a baking pan. Grill over a bed of hot coals for 1 hour. Remove from heat and cut a 4" hole in the top of the pumpkin. Scoop out the pulp and seeds and add to honey, fat, and corn drink. Return the mixture to the pumpkin. Replace the top, then baste the pumpkin with the drippings from the bottom of the dish. Grill an additional 35 minutes or until tender, basting occasionally. Serve whole, scooping out individual portions or cut into wedges. Ladle a little of the mixture over the pumpkin. Yields 6–8 servings.

Hickory Nut Bread

1 lb hickory nuts, crushed
1 c cornmeal
1 t salt
corn shucks, green
grape vine, green
water, boiling

Combine cornmeal, salt, and hickory nuts with a small amount of boiling water to make the ingredients stick together. Wrap in corn shucks, tying each bun securely with a vine. Place shucks in a large pot of boiling water over hot coals and cook until solid. Yields 4 servings.

Bread Fry

2 c cornmeal
water
1/2 c fat
1 t salt

Combine cornmeal, salt, and enough water to hold together. Shape into a round pone about the size of your pan and 1/8 " thick. Heat fat in pot over hot coals and fry pone until golden brown on both sides. Cut into wedges. Yields 4–6 servings.

Ribault found the Timucua to be friendly. They traded with the Indians, and the Indians, in turn, helped them. Saturiwa, Chief of the Timucua, and his tribesmen, even assisted the French in building Fort Caroline.

But the French were destined to be as unsuccessful as the early Spanish had been in La Florida. They were plagued with a lack of rations; illness overtook many, and angry tempers were common. It was during this difficult time for these French colonists that King Phillip II of Spain, determined to secure the trade route from the New World, commissioned Pedro Menéndez de Avilés to reclaim La Florida for the Spanish.

You will explore and colonize La Florida; and if there be settlers or corsairs of other nations not subject to us, drive them out.
  King Phillip II of Spain, 1565

Sixteenth Century Spanish Officer

Chapter II.
The First Spanish Period
1565-1763

On September 8, 1565, Pedro Menéndez de Avilés, with five ships, 200 sailors, 500 soldiers, and 100 settlers sailed into the River of Dolphins, near the Timucua village of Seloy. After disembarking, Menéndez planted the Spanish flag in the sandy soil near the present-day Nombre de Dios Mission. Having arrived on the birthday of the Catholic saint, Agustín, he named his new settlement San Agustín.

Menéndez and 400 men then marched 45 miles north to the French settlement at Fort Caroline. He was determined, under orders from the King of Spain, to purge the French, forever, from *La Florida*. Jean Ribault, who had set sail from Fort Caroline a few days earlier, was sailing south; both enemies were unaware of the other's movement. Several days later, when Menéndez and his soldiers descended on Fort Caroline, only a handful of men, women, and children escaped; those remaining at the fort were put to death or taken prisoner.

On his return to San Agustín, Menéndez learned that Ribault's ships had been wrecked south of San Agustín, in the vicinity of present-day Cape Canaveral, and that the French soldiers had been sighted marching north along the coast. Menéndez left immediately with 50 soldiers to locate Ribault. Twenty miles south of San Agustín, near an ocean inlet, Menéndez found Ribault and his men. They exchanged words across the narrow waterway until the French were convinced they would not be harmed if the Spanish ferried them over. As each group of ten was brought to the opposite shore, the French soldiers were led behind a sand dune and bound. After all 208 were on the Spanish side, the French were given food and water. Those who convinced the Spaniards that they had embraced Catholicism were spared; the French Huguenots, or Protestants, were executed. The waterway where the French Huguenots lost their lives and France lost its claim to La Florida was later named Matanzas, Spanish for "place of slaughter." It has retained that name through modern times as does the river that flows south from St. Augustine to that infamous channel.

With the defeat of Ribault and his brave compatriots, the fate of La Florida over the next 200 years was sealed. Menéndez's promise to colonize La Florida could now begin in earnest.

Since food shortages plagued the colonists, bread was used to thicken soups. Meats, when available, included beef, lamb, and especially pork. Spanish colonists hunted wild game and ate large quantities of fish although they always considered fish a poor man's diet. Garlic and olive oil were basic. Food sources also included cow and goat milk and their by-products, onions, a variety of beans, peas, squash, figs, and olives.

Originally brought to Spain by the Arabs, citrus, rice, and sugar cane were introduced to the New World

by the Spanish. In the New World the Spanish discovered potatoes, tomatoes, bell peppers, avocado, cocoa, and corn. Although the tomato may have been eaten in San Agustín during the First Spanish Period, research has not verified this. Water was not drunk consistently, since the Spanish generally drank wine or ale. Most of the spices they used came from the Orient: chili powder, pepper, saffron, cinnamon, cumin, mint, cilantro (coriander), and caraway. Other favorite spices were basil, dill, and mustard. The Spanish brought their use of salt with them. The paprika plant was discovered in the New World by the Spanish and dried to produce a pepper called pimentón, an authentic Spanish creation. The New World also gave the Spanish such delicacies as vanilla and chocolate.

Most early cooking incorporated potajes (or hotpots), cooking over a fire with a fireproof pole extended over the flame. Attached to the pole was a pot called an olla which held stews and soups. Cooking was also done over a charcoal fire using an iron pot atop a three legged trivet. The Spanish barbecued and roasted meat on spits and also smoked fish on a wooden grill, as taught by the Timucua. They used heated stones for baking breads and later advanced to building outdoor coquina ovens.

The Hispanic's most inventive method of cooking was the fogón. It originated in the Mediterranean and appeared in San Agustín sometime after the 1700s. A fogón was a coquina, waist high, stove for indoor use. It had two small openings on the top. On the front of the fogón were two openings under the top holes for building a small fire. When the day was calm, smoke from the fogón floated up and out of the house through a hole in the thatched roof. When the weather was windy, smoke filled the house.

The Metate-Basalt stone, in use between the 16th and 18th centuries.

Copper pots and earthenware accompanied the Spanish to the New World. They also brought iron knives and forks, wooden spoons, wooden stirrers, macaroni rollers, bone pastry wheels, and the ever-present Metate-Basalt stone for grinding corn.

The wealthy used silver bowls and utensils, ornate pottery, porcelain from the Orient, chocolate cups, and bone-handled utensils imported from England.

Pottery was imported from Spain or Mexico or made by the Timucua. The Spanish commoners ate from pewter or tin-washed copper plates or wooden bowls and drank from pewter mugs and black lead glaze cups. They used pewter, brass, or wooden spoons and pewter forks and knives for eating. Hand-blown glass bottles held rum, tinajas contained a variety of food products, and woven baskets, wooden barrels and boxes, casks, and canvas bags protected their food.

Meats and fish were preserved by salting, smoking, or curing with paprika. The practice of curing meat with paprika led to the origin of the famous Spanish chorizo sausage.

Oil was used to protect cheeses and sausages and vinegar and wine pickled vegetables and fruits. Sun-drying was also used for preserving fruits.

As early as the 1700s, ice was used by wealthy families in the English colonies. Enterprising individuals were cutting large blocks of ice from frozen ponds in

Spanish peasants

North America and then packing them in sawdust for transportation by ship. But La Florida had barely enough resources to provide food, much less purchase such a luxury as ice.

Sopas y Estofados

Soups and Stews

Unlike their predecessors, the Timucua, the Spanish were ill prepared for life in the New World. The hardships awaiting them were numerous, including heat, humidity, and mosquitoes. Dressed in impractical clothing, these men hunted unknown territory with a bulky black powder arquebus.

Arquebus

Often the men returned empty handed and disgruntled, unable to capture the fleet-footed white-tail deer as it lunged gracefully into the thickly vegetated swamp. Early Spanish writings indicate frustration with the governor of La Florida for not allowing the soldiers to follow wild game onto Indian land. But the Spaniards compensated for their lack of game with the cattle, goat, sheep, and swine that they brought to their new home.

By 1575, as friction with the Indians increased, the Spanish relocated San Agustín from Seloy to its present site. The tension, however, did not keep the Spanish and Timucua from accepting each other. In fact, many soldiers married Indian women.

Carne de Res Natosa
Creamed Beef

2 lbs beef, thinly sliced
1 med onion, chopped
3 T flour
1 c water
2 T salt
1 c red bell peppers, cored, diced
1 t paprika
2 cloves garlic, crushed
1 c cream
1 c kidney beans, cooked
1/4 c olive oil

Combine flour and seasonings in bowl. Dredge beef in mixture. Heat oil in pot and brown meat. Add remaining ingredients, except beans and cream. Cover pot and cook on low for 1 hour. Add beans and cook 15 minutes. Remove from heat and stir in cream. Yields 4 servings.

Chili Con Carne
Chili with Meat

2 lbs beef, ground
2 lg onions, chopped
2 cloves garlic, crushed
5 t brown sugar
4 c red kidney beans, cooked
2 t salt
4 t chili powder
1 T vinegar
2 bay leaves
1/8 c olive oil
1 c beef stock

In large pot brown onions and garlic in oil. Add meat and cook until brown. Add remaining ingredients and simmer for 1 hour. Yields 4 servings.

Sopa de Chili
Chili Soup

2 lbs beef, ground
4 c water
3 med onions, chopped
4 c potatoes, peeled, diced
3 green peppers, cored, chopped
3 t chili powder
1 T paprika
1 t salt
1 t pepper
1 c orange juice
1/4 c olive oil

In large pot brown beef, onions, salt, and pepper in oil. Drain off grease then add remaining ingredients to pot and simmer 1 hour. Yields 6 servings.

Estofado de Puerco
Pork Stew

4 lb pork roast, cubed
1 t salt
1 t pepper
3 cloves garlic, crushed
1 T cumin
1 red bell pepper, sliced
1/4 c olive oil
2 t saffron
1 c lime juice
2 c water
2 c raw rice, cooked

In a large pot heat oil and brown pork on all sides. Add remaining ingredients except rice and simmer 1 hour. Add rice to stew, blend, and serve. Yields 6-8 servings.

Albóndigas de Puerco
Pork Meatballs

2 c pork, ground
2/3 c milk
3/4 c bread crumbs
1/4 c olive oil
1 clove garlic, minced
1/4 c water
1 T paprika
1 egg
1/4 c cream

Combine milk and crumbs. Allow to stand until moisture is absorbed. Add garlic, paprika, egg, and pork. Blend thoroughly. Form into balls about 1-1/2" in diameter. Heat oil in pan. Add balls and cook through. Add water and cream, cover, and simmer 5 minutes. Yields about 3 dozen.

As a devout Catholic, one of Menéndez's objectives was to Christianize the Timucua. To further his mission, Jesuit priests were sent to La Florida. They were unsuited for the wild country, however, and eventually returned to Spain.

King Phillip II then sent a group of Franciscan friars to San Agustín. They were successful, establishing the first Franciscan Monastery in the New World.

Nombre de Dios Mission

Several walls of that monastery have been incorporated into the present-day St. Francis Barracks at 82 Marine Street.

A Franciscan priest, Father Pareja, converted hundreds of Timucua to Christianity. During the early 1600s, Father Pareja, a linguist, developed their language into a written form. Due to his efforts, the Timucuan language was among the first Native American languages to be systematically recorded and published in the New World.

Father Pareja had books printed for the Timucua, who mastered reading in an amazingly short period of time. A few examples of their language follow:

> **Cuiu yati?**
> Is there any fish?
>
> **Hetanicala.**
> Let's eat.
>
> **Tapola purunu puquacote.**
> What a lot of shelled corn!
>
> **Ucutamalaha.**
> They drink.

Preparing poultry: Pluck and clean fowl as soon as possible. Plucking is preferred to skinning as this enhances both flavor and appearance. Birds should be hung or aged before cooking. In some cases, aging makes a noticeable difference in the tenderness of the meat.
Hanging a bird simply means letting the fowl age, well wrapped, at room temperature for two days.

Sopa de Pollo
Chicken Soup

1 chicken
1 clove garlic, minced
1 t cinnamon
1 t salt
1 t thyme
8 c water
2 onions, diced
1 red bell pepper, cored, diced

Combine all ingredients in a large pot. Cover and bring to a boil. Reduce heat and simmer 1 hour or until chicken is done. Remove chicken from broth and discard skin and bones. Cut chicken into bite size pieces and return to broth. Simmer 15 minutes. Yields 4 servings.

"Pilau" de Pollo y Chorizo
Chicken and Sausage Pilau

Pilau, a variation of pilaf (from Turkey) is a dish of rice, meat, shellfish, or vegetables in a seasoned broth. Pronounced by Floridians as "perlo," it was brought to La Florida by the Spanish.

2 chickens, skinned, cut up
3 c rice
1 lb chorizo sausage, sliced
1 t salt
2 t saffron
1 T chili pepper
1 onion, diced
1 bell pepper, cored, diced
8 c water

Simmer chicken, salt, and chili pepper in water for 2 hours. Reserve liquid, remove chicken and debone. In liquid boil sausage 20 minutes, then remove from liquid. Measure broth.

Add more water so that you have 6 cups of liquid, then add chicken and remaining ingredients. Bring to a quick boil, then reduce heat and simmer 30 minutes. Yields 4-6 servings.

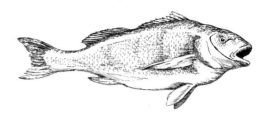

Pato y Puerco
Duck and Pork

2 ducks, halved
1/4 lb salt pork
1/4 c flour
8 potatoes, quartered
pod of red pepper
water

In a large pot fry out salt pork until light brown. Add red pepper and flour and slightly brown. Add ducks and cover with water. Cook 45 minutes on low heat. Add potatoes and cook an additional 45 minutes. Yields 4 servings.

In 1692, Jonathan Dickinson, his wife, their baby son, a few friends, and several slaves sailed from their homes in Jamaica bound for Philadelphia. They were shipwrecked near Jupiter Inlet, south of San Agustín, and captured by Ais Indians. The Indians, thinking their captives were Spanish, because a member of the party spoke Spanish, eventually led them to San Agustín. Dickinson later described his experiences.

. . . And sitting down by the wigwam . . . [an] Indian brought a fish boiled on a small palmetto leaf and set it down amongst us making signs for us to eat . . . .

Jonathan Dickinson, 1696

Pescado "Drum" Hervor
Boiled Drum Fish

2 lbs drum, filleted
4 slices bacon, cut into 1" strips
1 ham hock
3 onions, quartered
2 c black beans
2 c squash, diced
salt and pepper to taste
4 c water
1/2 c lime juice

In large pot combine all ingredients except the fish and squash. Cover and simmer 2 hours. Add squash and fish and simmer 20 minutes or until squash is tender. Yields 6 servings.

Pescado "Drum" Cremosa
Creamed Drum

1 lb drum, deboned
1 t pepper
1/4 c olive oil
1 sm bay leaf, crushed
1 t salt
1 onion, thinly sliced
1 clove garlic, minced
1 t saffron
1 t paprika
1 c corn
1/2 c cream

In a large pot, combine all ingredients, except cream. Simmer 30 minutes. Remove from heat and add cream. Yields 2 servings.

Castillo de San Marcos, built between 1672-1695. The coquina walls were originally stuccoed and whitewashed.

By the late 1500s, 300 men, women, and children inhabited primitive San Agustín. Although the soil was sandy and dry, gardens provided a meager variety of vegetables including squash, radishes, onions, peppers, watermelon, potatoes, and corn. However, fruit trees such as fig, cherry, peach, pomegranate, orange, grapefruit, lemon, and lime grew in abundance.

All remained relatively peaceful until 1586 when the English, led by Sir Francis Drake, sailed into Matanzas Bay, their ships' cannons roaring. The Spanish fled to the woods or nearby Indian villages while Drake's men burned the town to the ground. The Spanish returned to the ashes, rebuilt their houses, and replanted their gardens. As the years passed and San Agustín's population increased, its food supply decreased. Its gardens and its groves were now barely able to sustain the needs of the expanding military outpost.

In 1598, newly appointed Governor Menendez de Canzo, after surveying his outpost, wrote to the Spanish Monarchy that San Agustín would "build a plaza" named Plaza de Armas, the central plaza. The layout of the streets and the plaza for San Agustín followed the Spanish instructions for designing a town in the New World. At the eastern section of the plaza a marketplace was constructed where the first weights and measures system in the New World was introduced to assure fair trade.

For a hundred years, nine successive wooden forts protected San Agustín. But a second attack from the British in 1668 caused the military to build a more substantial fortification. Coquina from the King's quarry on Anastasia Island was selected for the building material. To supply labor, Indians were hired and African slaves were shipped from Cuba. On October 2, 1672 ground was broken for the Castillo de San Marcos. The scope of the project was phenomenal; food supplies, alone, created a serious problem. But the Spanish persevered and by 1695, 23 years later, the fort stood ready to protect San Agustín's population of over 1,500.

In 1702, seven years after the fort's completion, the bastion was tested. The English, under the command of South Carolina Governor James Moore, laid siege to the city while the townspeople sought refuge in the fort. The fort was well prepared for such a crisis as the military had dug several deep wells for drinking water and had stored large quantities of food.

The thick coquina walls of the Castillo withstood the impact of British cannon-balls for 50 days. Food was rationed and tempers flared, but the Spanish prevailed. South Carolina Governor Moore, concluding that the fort was impenetrable, ordered the town burned before setting sail for the Carolinas.

For a second time, San Agustín was rebuilt. However, the continued threat of invasion from the British colonies to the north finally caused the Spanish to increase fortification of the city. They constructed the Cubo Line in 1704, a wall of palmetto logs running from the fort west to the San Sebastian River along present-day Orange Street.

The Rosario Line, completed in 1719, extended south from the Cubo Line down present-day Cordova Street and Maria Sanchez Creek. It then turned due east and followed present-day San Salvador Street adjacent to the National Cemetery on Marine Street to the Matanzas River, a favorite habitat for the high-jumping mullet.

Pescado "Mullet"
Mullet

The best way to capture the prized mullet is to toss a weighted net into the water and pull in a full load.

4 lbs mullet, split down the middle
2 lg onions, diced
2 lg bell peppers, cored, diced
2 lg red peppers, cored, diced
3 cloves garlic, minced
salt and pepper to taste
3 T vinegar
6 T olive oil
2 c rice
4 c beef stock
2 t saffron

In a large pot heat oil and lightly brown mullet, turning once. Add ingredients and simmer, covered, 45 minutes. Yields 6-8 servings.

During a "friendly" visit to San Agustín, General James Oglethorpe of the English colony of Georgia, was unimpressed with what he observed.

> . . . the place produces nothing but a few pomkings and Squashes & Small beans . . . .
>
> James Oglethorpe, 1743

Little changed after almost 20 years from General Oglethorpe's visit. A priest reporting to the Spanish Crown regarding food supplies wrote:

> The citizenry maintain themselves most of the year with salted meat, fish which abound in the rivers, and some vegetables.
>
> Father Juan José Solano, 1759

Estofado de Frijoles
Bean Stew

3 c kidney beans, cooked
3 slices bread, toasted, cubed
1 clove garlic, crushed
1/2 c olive oil
salt and pepper to taste
1 med onion, chopped
8 c milk

In a large pot brown onions and garlic in oil. Add beans and milk and bring to a quick boil. Stir in bread and spices. Yields 6-8 servings.

After completion of the Castillo de San Marcos—and realizing there was still an abundant supply of coquina on nearby Anastasia Island, the governor granted permission for the public to use the material. Stones were ferried across the Matanzas River to construct homes, government buildings, and the fogón for cooking. Coquina buildings soon replaced earlier wooden huts giving the town a more substantial appearance.

An expansion of the original Government House, which had been erected around 1598, occurred by 1706. Located at 48 King Street, adjacent to the town's public market, the ground floor of Government House was made of coquina; its second story of wood. Perfect for entertaining, the spacious rooms had high ceilings to capture the ocean breeze. Behind the building grew a wide variety of fruit trees.

Estofado de Camarón
Shrimp Stew

2 lbs shrimp
20 c water
4 onions, quartered
4 bell peppers, cored, quartered
4 cloves garlic
4 potatoes, peeled, halved
4 ears of corn
4 t chili powder
2 lemons, halved
1/4 c salt

Boil water, spices, and lemons for 10 minutes. Add potatoes and boil 10 minutes more. Add corn, peppers, and onions, and boil 10 minutes. Add shrimp and boil until they turn pink. Drain. Yields 4 servings.

Jagged-edged oysters are accessible in estuaries during low tide. Harvesting them should always be undertaken with caution. Wear protective footwear and gloves and take along a hammer and large cloth bag or basket.

A modern-day problem arising from oyster harvesting is the possibility of contamination from effluent runoff. Contact the health department to be sure that the oyster bed you use is free of harmful bacteria. Also, remember that oysters should be harvested only during the months which have an "**R**" in them, as generally those are the months when both the weather and the water are cool.

January, February, March
April, September, October
November, December

Once you've harvested a bushel or two, clean thoroughly under running water to wash away the mud. To shuck oysters wear gloves and pry open the shell with a round-tip knife. Better yet, use a commercial oyster knife which has a short, thick handle and short, round-tip blade.

Estofado de Ostiones
Oyster Stew

4 c oysters, shucked
4 c water
1 c cream
1/4 lb salt pork, diced, cooked until crisp
salt and pepper to taste

Bring all ingredients, except cream, to a boiling point. Reduce heat and simmer 15 minutes. Add cream and simmer 5 minutes. Yields 4 servings.

Ensaladas
Salads

Seville and Valencia oranges, lemons, limes, and grapefruit were brought to the New World by the Spanish. The soil and the climate were obviously perfect for such a venture because the Spanish shipped barrels of fruit back to their native land. By the 1700s orange groves were so plentiful throughout San Agustín that 28,000 oranges were also shipped to the British colony of Charleston, South Carolina. It is interesting to note that the Spanish considered ensaladas to be cheap foods for the lower class society.

La Valencia
The Valencia

3 Valencia oranges, sectioned
2 grapefruit, sectioned
3 T olive oil
1/4 t salt
1/4 t cinnamon
1 T brown sugar

Place fruit sections in bowl and sprinkle with spices. Pour oil over fruit and mix thoroughly. Yields 4 servings.

Frutas de Menéndez
Menéndez Fruit

The pomegranate, a favorite fruit of the Timucua, was also enjoyed by the Spanish. Its rich pulp and dark red juice were used for flavoring. Pomegranate extract is known as grenadine.

1 c oranges, sectioned
1 c hickory nuts, chopped
1 c pomegranates, sliced
1 c coconut, shredded
1 c cherries, pitted, sliced
1 c bananas, sliced
1/2 c cream, soured

Combine all ingredients and toss lightly. Yields 6-8 servings.

Ensalada de Aguacate
Avocado Salad

Considered an aphrodisiac by the Aztec, the avocado is native to the New World, deriving its name from the corrupted Aztec "ahuacatl." Today's markets generally sell this "alligator pear," as it is nicknamed, before it is ripe. To hasten the ripening process place the fruit in a brown paper bag.

Salad:
3 avocados, peeled, sliced
2 oranges, sectioned
2 c grapes, seeds removed

Dressing:
3 slices bacon
1/4 c lemon juice
1 t sugar
1 orange rind, grated

Salad: Combine all ingredients and toss lightly.

Dressing: Fry bacon until crisp. Drain and pat dry. Reserve grease. Dissolve sugar in hot grease. Add lemon juice and bring to a quick boil. Add rind, stir well, then drizzle over salad. Yields 6-8 servings.

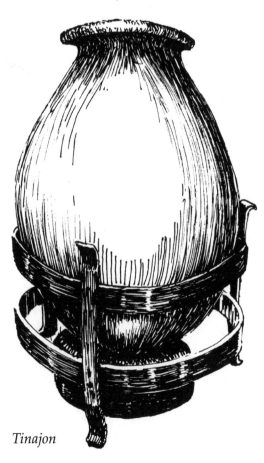

Tinajon

A tinajon is an earthen jar that comes in various sizes, sometimes as tall as four feet. It was used to ship food supplies to La Florida from Spain. Water for the sailors at sea, flour, or olives floating in salty brine, were contained in each jar, its contents ready to supply the needs of San Agustín.

Ensalada Franciscana
Franciscan Salad

3 c grapefruit, sectioned
1 c oranges, sectioned
1 c peaches, sliced
1/2 c honey

Blend all ingredients carefully so as not to bruise fruit. Yields 4 servings.

Ensalada de Ajo y Aceitunas
Garlic Olive Salad

2 T olive oil
1/4 t paprika
1 T caraway seed
1 clove garlic, minced
1 c Spanish olives, pimento-stuffed

Combine oil, garlic, paprika, and caraway. Toss with olives. Remove garlic prior to serving. Yields 1 cup.

During the First Spanish Period, corn and kidney beans were the most abundant staples of the common folk of San Agustín. They seasoned their vegetables with red peppers, garlic, and onions.

Frijoles en Escabeche
Beans Vinaigrette

1 c kidney beans, cooked
1 c garbanzo beans, cooked

1 lg onion, thinly sliced
1 red pepper,
 thinly sliced
1 c red wine
 vinegar
1/2 c Spanish
 olives, sliced
1/2 c olive oil
1/2 c sugar
1/4 t chili
 powder
1/2 t salt
1 T pepper

Olive jar

In a jar with a lid, blend vinegar, sugar, oil, and spices. In a separate bowl combine remaining ingredients. Pour dressing over and toss carefully. Yields 6-8 servings.

Cebollas en Escabeche
Onions Vinaigrette

4 c onions, thinly sliced
1 t salt
2 c red wine vinegar
2 cloves garlic, minced
1/2 c sugar
1 t pepper

Combine all ingredients, except onions, in a pot. Bring to a boil then drop in onions. Remove from heat and allow to cool. Yields 6 servings.

Dulces
Sweets

While the common folk of San Agustín ate mostly starches, the government offi- *cials and moneylenders imported expensive delicacies such as vanilla and chocolate from Spain. The Spanish discovered these flavors when they conquered the Aztecs of Mexico. Catholic priests considered eating chocolate to be a sin because it was so delicious. Their point of view gave rise to cakes made with chocolate being called "Devil's Food."*

Pudín de Chocolate
Chocolate Pudding

Pudding Mixture:
1 egg
1 c sugar
2 t butter
6 T unsweetened chocolate, grated
1-3/4 c flour, sifted
1 t salt
1/4 t cream of tartar
1/4 t baking soda
1 c milk
water

Hard Sauce:
1 stick butter, softened
1 c sugar
1 egg white
1/4 c rum
1 t cinnamon, ground

Pudding: In mixing bowl, beat egg, sugar, butter, and chocolate. Sift together flour, salt, tartar, and soda. Beat in dry ingredients alternately with milk. Pour into buttered top of a double boiler. Cover. Place water in bottom of double boiler and bring to a boil. Reduce heat and steam 2 hours. Add more water to bottom of pot if necessary. If pudding is sticky when done, place in a warm oven for a few minutes.

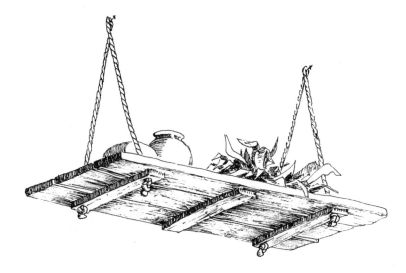

There were no cupboards attached to the walls of early Spanish homes. Cupboards and shelf space in those days meant higher taxes. So in order to protect food from scurrying creatures, ropes were suspended from the ceiling to which wide planks were attached.

This created a swinging table several feet above the food preparation table which was located in the living area. Net cloths were also used to protect food. But the ever present and most resourceful palmetto bug still found ways to locate a meal.

Sauce: Cream butter and sugar until very light. Add egg white and continue to beat. Add rum a little at a time, beating until very fluffy. Pour sauce over pudding then sprinkle with cinnamon. Yields 4-6 servings.

Dulce de Coco
Coconut Candy

3 c sugar
1/2 c coconut milk
2 coconuts, shelled, grated
1 T vanilla
olive oil

In pot, combine all ingredients except oil. Blend well, then simmer until thick, stirring occasionally. Using a teaspoon, form small balls and place on an oiled pan. After the candy har-

dens, store in a covered container. Yields approximately 4 dozen.

Los Panes

Bread

Bread was an important staple for the Spanish, especially ashcakes prepared daily by the women of San Agustín. Toward the end of the 1500s, the Governor ordered a horse-drawn grist mill built in the Plaza de Armas to relieve the women from the daily chore of hand-grinding corn on their Metate-Basalt stones.

When soldiers at the fort were issued their daily ration of el pan, they ate it dipped in a combination of olive oil and vinegar, accompanied by radishes and onions.

When times were hard and food scarce, the soldiers were reduced to eating baked "hardtack," a combination of flour, often stale, a little salt, lard, and water. For years local citizens bid at public auctions held on the steps of the Government House to win a contract to supply bread for the soldiers at the fort.

Tortita de Maíz
Corncakes

1 c cornmeal
1/2 t salt
1/2 c flour
1/2 c milk
1 egg
1/2 c water
1 t baking powder
1/4 c olive oil

Mix together all ingredients except oil. Mold into thin cakes and set aside. Heat oil in skillet until hot then add cakes and fry until lightly browned. Yields 4 servings.

Cornmeal

Bizcocho Agrio
Sour Biscuits

1/2 c cornmeal
1 egg, beaten
4 strips bacon, fried, reserve drippings
1 t salt
1 t sugar
1 c milk, soured by adding 1 T vinegar

1/4 t soda
1 t water
1/2 c water, boiling

Sift cornmeal in baking dish then add bacon, bacon drippings, sugar, and salt. Pour in boiling water, stir well then set aside to cool. In separate bowl combine egg, milk, soda, and 1 t water, and mix well. Bake at 350° for 30 minutes or until set. Yields 4 servings.

Pan de Calabaza
Squash Bread

2 c squash, grated
1 c hickory nuts, chopped
2 c sugar
3 eggs
1 c olive oil
3 c flour
1/4 t baking powder
1 t salt
1 t soda
1 t cinnamon

Beat sugar, eggs, and oil until well blended. Sift dry ingredients together then stir slowly into mixture. Add squash and nuts and stir until well blended. Pour into 2 greased bread pans and bake at 350° for 40 minutes or until brown. Yields 2 loaves.

Pan de Frijol
Bean Bread

2 c milk, scalded
1/2 c sugar
2 eggs, beaten
1 T salt
1 c kidney beans, cooked, mashed
1/2 c olive oil
8 c flour or more

2 pkg yeast dissolved in 1/2 c warm
  water

In pot combine oil, sugar, and salt. Add milk and stir well. Blend in beans then heat to lukewarm. Add prepared yeast then eggs and mix well. Pour into bowl then add flour and knead until smooth. Cover and let rise until double in bulk. Punch down, shape into 24 balls, cover, and let rise again. When doubled in size place on ungreased pan and bake at 350° for 20 to 25 minutes. Yields approximately 2 dozen.

During the 1730s the Spanish crown offered freedom to all African slaves escaping from the British colonies, if they would join the Catholic Church and declare their allegance to the King of Spain. Many slaves heard of this offer and made their way on the first "underground railroads" from the British colonies into Spanish Florida.

The first free community for ex-slaves in America was named Gracia Real de Santa Teresa de Mose, or Fort Mose, settled in 1739, two miles north of the Castillo. It was short-lived, however, for in 1740, the British, under the command of Georgia's General James Oglethorpe, attacked San Agustín and Fort Mose was destroyed.

Once again the townspeople fled to the safety of the massive Castillo de San Marcos. The Spanish were near starvation when supplies from Cuba were finally slipped safely into the harbor. General Oglethorpe, unable to capture the supplies or the fort, withdrew in defeat, admitting that the Castillo de San Marcos simply could not be taken.

Bebidas

Beverages

The high water table in San Agustín made the digging of wells a simple task. However, assuring clean water from those wells was difficult whether the wells were made of barrel or coquina. To solve the "murky" issue, enterprising settlers used lava rock—ballast from their ships—to clarify water for drinking. First, they carved out a bowl in the top of the lava rock called a "pila."

After drawing water from the well, they transferred it to the porous lava rock for filtering and purification. The muddy water would then drain through the rock to the awaiting clay pot as clear water, ready for drinking.

Besides water and several other popular beverages, the Timucuan Indians' favorite beverage, the caffeine-rich "Black Drink," was also a favorite among the Spanish.

Coctel Picante San Agustín
St. Augustine Spicy Cocktail

4 c squash, finely chopped
1/2 c malt vinegar
1 green pepper, cored, finely chopped
1/2 c rum
1 Spanish onion, finely chopped
1 t salt
2 T sugar
2 T red pepper, cored, finely chopped
1 T black pepper

Combine all ingredients and stir until well blended. Serve with a spoon. Yields 4-6 servings.

Sangría
Wine Punch

8 c red wine
1 c water
16 T sugar
8 cloves, whole
16 T allspice
2 T cinnamon
16 T lemon juice
2 c orange juice
1 orange, thinly sliced
1 apple, cut in eighths

Simmer spices, water, sugar, stirring occasionally. Cool then add remaining ingredients. Yields 10-14 servings.

Pila

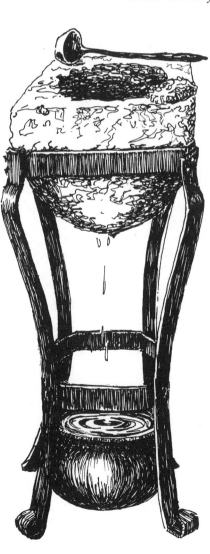

Jugo de Frutas La Florida
Florida Fruit Punch

6 c orange juice
4 c lemon juice
2 T cloves, whole
1 T allspice, whole
3 c water
1/2 t salt
6 cinnamon sticks
1 c brown sugar

Combine all the ingredients in a large pot. Simmer for 2 hours. Yields 10-14 servings.

From the earliest days of San Agustín's settlement in 1565, the outpost was almost totally dependent on Cuba and Spain for provisions. After the English colonized North America in 1607, the Spanish also relied on them for supplies and food they were unable to produce in La Florida. When San Agustín's supplies were depleted by English invasions and plunderings, the governors of San Agustín often resorted to privateering.

Government officials, as well as the soldiers of the Castillo, were also dependent on the Crown for financial support. This government subsidy to its colonies was Spain's "situado." Soldiers were promised pay for guarding the town, but money was slow in coming, if it arrived at all.

Colonists complained of their conditions to Spanish officials. They were weary, often starving and embittered. They had lost much of their enthusiasm for colonizing paradise. In fact, the Spanish settlers had become so disenchanted with life in the New World that they petitioned the Crown to relocate the San Agustín outpost to her sister city, short-lived Santa Elena, which had been established on what is now Parris Island, South Carolina.

Their complaining and petitioning did nothing to alter the attitude of the King of Spain. After all, Spain was gaining in riches and power, having pillaged the proud Incas of South America, the Mayans of Central America, and the Aztecs of Mexico.

The Spanish Crown wanted its treasure laden vessels protected as they sailed up the coast of La Florida on their way home to Spain. For this reason the Crown informed San Agustín's citizens that they would remain in La Florida.

Spanish Quarter Restoration

Chapter III.
The British and the Minorcans
1763-1783

*I*n 1763, the First Treaty of Paris ended the Seven Years' War, known in America as the French and Indian War. Florida, which extended west to the Mississippi River, was ceded by Spain to England in return for Spain's prized port city, Havana, Cuba. France lost Canada to England and all lands west of the Mississippi to Spain. This restructuring of political domination in the New World brought great resentment from *La Florida's* Spanish population. Most of them had lived their entire lives in San Agustín. But there seemed to be little pity for the Spanish. When the British arrived they accused the Spanish of laziness. A British representative sent to inspect the colony reported that the town had little food, noting that there was an abundance of fish, but no vegetables.

The Spanish flag was lowered from the ramparts of the Castillo de San Marcos, the British flag unfurled, and the old Spanish fort renamed Fort St. Marks. The town's population of 3,000, including 95 free Negroes who had reestablished themselves at Fort Mose, 315 Negro slaves, 89 Christian Timucuan Indians, and roughly 2,500 Spaniards prepared to vacate San Agustín for Havana. Abandoned were 300 houses and various personal possessions. Only a few Spaniards chose to remain.

The proud Timucua, who had numbered over 25,000 when the Spanish arrived in 1565, had been ravaged by disease, slaughtered or kidnapped by enemy tribes or the English, or taken to Cuba as slaves. Much to the concern of the British, a new group arrived: the Lower Creek Indians, later to be called the Seminoles.

England divided Florida into east and west to be governed as two separate entities. In the west, George Johnstone was appointed Governor at Pensacola, a small Spanish military outpost along the Gulf of Mexico. James Grant of Scotland was chosen to govern East Florida. Its capital, San Agustín, was renamed St. Augustine. When Grant took leadership at St. Augustine it was no more than a mile long by a quarter of a mile wide. Governor Grant described the hamlet as a "rather dull little place," but set about to change that condition. Known for his large size and equally large appetite for food and entertainment, Governor Grant turned listless St. Augustine into a social community. During his first year in office, official records indicated that he and his guests consumed:

four barrels of beef
two barrels of pork
four barrels of rice
twelve barrels of flour
turtles
fish
venison
oysters
turkeys
chickens
ducks
capons
hams
bacon
lamb

Meats were a necessity for the English, especially lamb. They also hunted wild game and harvested seafood. They ate the same types of vegetables and fruits as did the Spanish, supplemented by large quantities of potatoes and rice. Milk and cheese from goats and cows were also favorites.

Seminoles made their favorite corn drink, "soft-kin," from corn which had been parched, ground, or soaked in a variety of meats, nuts, or wood chips. The Seminoles' diet paralleled that of the Timucua, but the Seminoles later learned to enjoy the meats and vegetables of the English.

The British generally drank ciders, ales, and tea. With their talent for gardening, they grew a wide assortment of spices including caraway, thyme, mint, geranium, dill, rosemary, marjoram, fennel, yarrow, tarragon, basil, chamomile, ginger, and parsley.

Wooden
Spice and
Tobacco
Rack

The British built indoor fireplaces for both warmth and cooking. A sturdy iron hook was imbedded in the side of the fireplace for holding cooking pots. A primitive technique for roasting joints of meat or fowl was to suspend the food in front of the fire by a hemp rope tied to a peg in the ceiling. Someone would be appointed to turn the roast as needed. Usually it would be an unwilling child or a slave.

Salt-glazed stoneware, wooden bowls, iron, pewter, brass, and copper pots were fashioned. Long-handled spoons were made of wood, iron, or pewter. Cutting knives were cast from iron.

Most iron cooking containers had three or four legs so they could sit more securely on the floor near or in the flames. These included pots, kettles, skillets, and gridirons. The British also had toasting forks, waffle irons, baking kettles, and the Dutch oven (created by the Dutch), which was oblong with a door in the front. This crafty cooking device sat near the flame. The meat inside could be conveniently basted by opening the door. Revolving churns, barrel churns, cheese presses, and spice mills had been in use for some time in the English colonies and were introduced into Florida by the British.

Pewter, salt-glaze stoneware, creamware, porcelain plates from China, and fine English bone china cups and saucers were used. Silver forks, spoons, and mugs were accessible for the wealthy. Clear or green hand-blown wine glasses were owned by the more affluent. Mugs for the common folk were usually crafted from pewter or creamware.

Salting and smoking continued to be the primary means for preserving meats and fish. Wealthy families often built separate smoke houses for processing beef, hams, and fish. Drying was popular as was pickling vegetables, fruits, and berries. Fruits and their blossoms were also candied or made into marmalade or preserves. Ice remained unavailable in Florida.

Game, Meat, and Fowl

The public slaughtering pen used by St. Augustine's residents was located near the town gate. Game and cattle were brought there for dressing before being carted off to market at the Plaza, half a mile to the south.

Stewed Cooter and White-tail

The soft-shell turtle, or cooter, as it is called in Florida, has a vicious temper, but is excellent eating. When attempting to capture one, handle it from the rear of the shell to save your fingers from its sharp beak.

3 lbs turtle meat, sliced
3 c beef stock
2 lbs deer, cubed
1/4 c tarragon
3 c milk
4 onions, sliced
2 T marjoram
1/4 c lard
salt and pepper to taste

Drop cooter into boiling water. Remove when dead, cut meat, and discard remaining turtle. In large kettle brown turtle and venison in lard. Combine with remaining ingredients, except milk, and simmer for 2 hours. Add milk and heat thoroughly. Yields 6-8 servings.

English Beef Liver with Onions

1 lb beef liver, thinly sliced
1 T salt
1 onion, sliced
1/4 c butter
1/2 c bread crust, crumbled
2 c water
salt and pepper to taste

Place liver, salt, and water in iron pot. Boil until water is almost gone then remove meat and discard water. To the pot add butter and onion and fry until onion is light brown. Remove onions from pot and place on plate. Put liver back into pot and fry, adding a bit more oil if needed. When brown, add onion, season with salt and pepper. Serve with a little mound of onion on top of each piece of meat. Top each onion with bread crumbs. Yields 2 servings.

Beef Stew

2 lbs beef, cubed
4 potatoes, cubed
4 carrots, thickly sliced
4 onions, quartered
2 c beef stock
2 t sugar
2 t salt
2 T flour
1/4 c lard
1 T thyme

In a large kettle brown meat in lard. Add remaining ingredients and stir. Cover and simmer 1 hour. Yields 4-6 servings.

Shortly after the English took possession of Florida, Captain Joseph Peavett, of the British Militia, and his wife, Mary, purchased what is now known as the Oldest House. This enterprising couple added a second floor for their private living quarters and two rooms downstairs for a tavern and store. They built a fireplace inside for heating and cooking, a rarity for Spanish San Agustín. The Peavetts not only fed the officers from across the street at the St. Francis Barracks, but they rented them rooms as well. Archaeological excavations confirm that the site of this house has been continuously occupied since the early 1600s.

The Oldest House

The Oldest House was acquired by the St. Augustine Historical Society in 1918 and was designated a National Historic Landmark in 1970. Located at 14 St. Francis Street, it is open daily for tours of the museum, house, and gardens.

British Silver Ladle, dated 1770

Captain Peavett's Lamb Bake

1-1/2 lbs lamb, cubed
1/2 lb prunes, pitted
1 c water, boiling
4 T lard
2 med onions, chopped
2 cloves garlic, minced
1 t salt
1 t pepper
1 t rosemary
1 t thyme
1 bay leaf, crushed
1 c beef stock
2 lg carrots, thickly sliced
2 lg potatoes, diced
12 green olives, pitted
1 med orange, thinly sliced
1 t parsley, chopped

Boil prunes for 15 minutes or until they are plump. In skillet combine lard, onions, and garlic and brown. Add meat and brown, stirring all the while. Add seasonings, stir, and simmer for 12 minutes. Add stock, cover, and simmer for 1 hour. Add carrots and potatoes and simmer an additional 15 minutes. Add remaining ingredients, except parsley, and simmer 15 more minutes. Sprinkle with parsley. Yields 4-6 servings.

Militia Lamb Hash with Poached Eggs

Meat mixture:
1-1/2 lbs lamb, cooked, diced
4 T butter
1 med onion, chopped
1 clove garlic, crushed
1/2 red bell pepper, cored, finely chopped
2 lg potatoes, cooked, diced
1 t nutmeg
1 t salt
1 t pepper
1/2 lb peas, cooked

Eggs:
2 c water
1 t malt vinegar
4 eggs
1 t salt

Meat mixture: Melt butter in a large pan then add onion and brown. Add garlic and peppers. Cook 6-7 minutes, stirring and mashing. Add remaining ingredients, except peas, and mix well. Pour into a casserole dish, cover, and bake for 20 minutes at 350°. When mixture has cooked, place hash on a dish and add peas. Keep warm while cooking eggs.

Eggs: In a saucepan, combine water, salt, and vinegar and bring to a boil. Reduce heat then break eggs, one at a time, into a small bowl, and slide into the saucepan. Allow to simmer 2-3 minutes. Make sure that egg whites are solid. When eggs are done, use a slotted spoon and gently lift eggs from saucepan and onto hash. Yields 4 servings.

General Oglethorpe's Wine Pork

2 lbs pork, cubed
1/4 c lard
1 bay leaf
1/2 t sage
1 c onion, chopped
1/4 t thyme
2 c mushrooms, thickly sliced
3 T lard
3 T flour
2 c carrots, thinly sliced
1 c chicken broth
1-1/4 c Port wine
1/4 t pepper
2 cloves garlic, sliced

Heat lard in iron pot and brown pork. Remove meat and add onion and garlic. Brown until golden. Add flour and stir for 1 minute. Then add 1 c wine, bay leaf, broth, and remaining spices. Boil and stir until mixture thickens. Stir in meat and cover. Simmer 1 hour, stirring once. Add carrots, cover, and simmer 30 minutes. Add a bit of water if needed. In separate pan brown mushrooms in lard until golden. Add remaining wine to pan, stir, then add to pot. Gently stir then simmer, covered, for 3 minutes. Yields 6 servings.

Seville Orange-Baked Chicken Breast

4 chicken breasts, skinned, deboned
1 c onion, minced
2/3 c flour
1/2 c lard
4 T hickory nuts, chopped
4 t salt
4 T pimento, chopped
1 T pepper
3 T lemon juice
2 c rice
4 c water
2 T Seville orange rind, grated

Rinse chicken and pat dry. Mix flour, half of salt and pepper, and coat meat. In an iron kettle brown chicken in lard then remove. To the same kettle add all remaining ingredients except rice. Stir well then add rice and arrange chicken on top. Cover kettle and bake for 40 minutes at 350°. Remove lid then bake an additional 15 minutes. Yields 4 servings.

Capon with Scuppernong Grapes

The scuppernong grape, which ripens in late summer, is native to Florida. It is thick-skinned, very sweet, and has a yellowish or purple skin. If you want to pick them, you'll have to fight the Blue Jays.

4 capon breasts
1 c scuppernongs, seeds and skin removed
1/2 t salt
1/2 t pepper
1/2 c butter
1/2 c rum
1/3 c orange marmalade
1/2 c orange juice
1/4 t cinnamon
2-1/2 T orange rind, grated

Rub capon with salt and pepper. In large kettle brown capon in butter, turning occasionally, about 10 minutes. Cover and roast 15 minutes at 350°. Remove capon from kettle. Stir drippings in kettle to loosen. Add remaining ingredients, except grapes and orange rind, and stir well. Simmer until the sauce has thickened slightly and is dark in color, about 10 minutes. Add 1/2 of the grapes then return capon to kettle and cook in sauce until just heated through. To serve, first spoon some of the sauce onto each plate. Place 1 breast on each plate then garnish with grapes and orange rind. Yields 4 servings.

In St. Augustine, the legend suggests that the famous datil pepper was introduced into the New World by the Minorcans, a group of indentured colonists who sailed from Minorca to New Smyrna, Florida, in 1768. Others suggest that the datil pepper was not grown in the area until the next century.

Promised land and eventual freedom by the Scottish physician Andrew Turnbull, in exchange for years of farming, the Minorcans, accompanied by a few Greeks and Italians, experienced only misery and unproductive backbreaking labor.

After losing more than half of the original 1,400 Minorcan colonists to disease and starvation, those remaining abandoned their meager farms and servitude and in 1777 trudged the more than 60 miles north to St. Augustine, bringing with them hearty foods and their waxy, yellow-green red hot datil pepper. Today, St. Augustine is the only place in the United States where the datil pepper is grown abundantly, raised commercially, and shipped internationally.

Warning: When you bite into a datil pepper and your mouth begins to burn, reach for dairy products, sugar, or carrot juice to cool the heat—not water, as it only intensifies the pain.

Datil Pepper

Grilled Datil Pepper Chicken

3 lbs chicken, skinned, cut up
1 t salt
1 clove garlic, minced
2 T datil pepper, crushed
2 lemons, thinly sliced
1 red bell pepper, cored, thinly sliced
1 bell pepper, cored, thinly sliced
4 T olive oil
1 c chicken broth

Grunt

Fish and Seafood

Put chicken and broth in an iron pot. Sprinkle with salt and datil pepper. Place peppers over chicken then add garlic. Arrange lemon slices on top then pour oil over top. Cover and bake at 350° for 50-60 minutes or until chicken is thoroughly cooked. Yields 6 servings.

Guana Wild Turkey Pie

1 turkey breast, deboned, sliced
4 med potatoes, halved
4 med carrots, sliced
2 red peppers, cored, diced
1/2 c mushrooms, sliced
1 c cream
salt and pepper to taste
parsley
1/4 c lard

Grease a roasting pan. Arrange turkey at one end of pan. Next to turkey place potatoes, then the carrots. Sprinkle red peppers and mushrooms over all then season with salt and pepper. Pour cream over top then generously sprinkle with parsley. Cover and bake at 350° for 1 hour or until turkey and vegetables are tender. Add additional parsley if desired. Yields 6 servings.

The Minorcans kept to themselves during the English Period. However, their fishing skills contributed to the overall economy of St. Augustine. The Spanish had long considered fish to be the poor man's diet; it was no different with the destitute Minorcans.

Grilled Ocean Trout

8 trout, filleted
2 T butter
1/2 t salt
1/4 t pepper
2 eggs, hard cooked, finely chopped
2 eggs, well beaten
1/4 c milk
2 T datil pepper, finely chopped
2 lemons, thinly sliced
1-1/2 c bread crumbs

Salt and pepper trout. Mix raw eggs and milk. Dip trout into mixture, then roll gently in bread crumbs. Grease grill so fish won't stick. Make a paste of the butter, cooked eggs, and datil pepper and set aside. Cook fish on grill until golden in color, about 5-6 minutes on each side. Remove to platter. Spread paste over each fillet and top each with 2 slices of lemon. Yields 8 servings.

St. Augustine Lime Snapper

2 lbs snapper, filleted
1/2 c green onions, chopped
1 lime peel, grated
1/4 c olive oil
1 t salt
1 T pepper
3 T parsley, chopped
3 limes, thinly sliced
1 clove garlic, minced
2 squash, thinly sliced

Brown onions and garlic in oil until slightly brown. Add lime peel, pepper, salt, and parsley. Mix well. Bring to a boil, reduce heat, then simmer for 5 minutes. Add fish and squash. Simmer, covered for 8-10 minutes. Drain then garnish with lime slices. Yields 2-4 servings.

Although flounder can be caught with hook and line, gigging at night is more fun. Flounder rests on the bottom of estuaries so finding them is a hide and seek game. Before the invention of lanterns and flashlights, a heart-of-pine or "fat lighter" torch was dipped in oil and lit, creating illumination.

If you go alone, the gig or pronged spear, is carried in one hand, the torch in the other. But it's more practical to take a buddy. Wade along the shore in knee deep water and if your eyes are keen and the light is right, you can see the outline of the flounder. By the way, flounder gigging can also be done in broad daylight, but it's not as challenging.

Baked Matanzas Inlet Flounder

4 lb flounder, filleted
1 c water
1 c potatoes, peeled, thinly sliced
1 onion, thinly sliced
4 slices salt pork
1/2 c flour
1 T salt
1 T pepper

Rub fish with salt, pepper, and flour. Place in a baking dish and cover with water. Add vegetables then top with salt pork. Bake at 350° for 45 minutes. Yields 4 servings.

Stewed Oysters English Style

4 c oysters, sliced
3 slices salt pork, cubed
6 med potatoes, peeled, cubed
1 onion, diced
salt and pepper to taste
water

In large pot fry salt pork until crisp. Drain grease and add remaining ingredients. Cover with water and simmer for 45 minutes, covered. Yields 2-4 servings.

Florida Seafood Soup

1 lb fish, filleted, cut in chunks
1/2 lb shrimp, peeled
2 c oysters
4 c water
1 datil pepper, diced
1 c red wine
2 T olive oil
1 T lemon juice
1/4 c flour
1 bay leaf

1 c onion, diced
1 t salt
1 clove garlic, minced

In large pot heat olive oil. Slowly blend in flour, stirring constantly until mixture is light brown. Add onion, pepper, and garlic, and continue stirring until vegetables are tender. Gradually stir in water. Add remaining ingredients except seafood. Bring to a boil then simmer 10 minutes. Add fish and simmer 10 minutes longer. Add shrimp and oysters and cook for 10 minutes. Yields 8 servings.

Iron Trivet and Cooking Pot

Since Governor James Grant believed St. Augustine was suitable for the agrarian plantation system, he established "Grant's Villa" near the site of old Fort Mose. Ironically, the former site of the first free African community in the New World became home to over 48 slaves who were brought from Africa to farm his 300 acres. Other planters from the Carolina colony followed his example, including John Moultrie who settled south of St. Augustine near present-day Moultrie Creek, naming his plantation "Bella Vista." John Moultrie became acting governor of East Florida when Governor Grant, suffering from gout, left Florida for England in 1771. During the 20 years that England ruled Florida, its agricultural ventures were a success. St. Augus-

tine exported indigo, rice, over 65,000 oranges, and hundreds of barrels of orange juice.

Former Governor Grant later wrote favorably of his stay in the town.

> *The Winter is so remarkable temperate that vegetables of every kind are raised during that season without any Art. The Soil on the Coast is in general Sandy but productive with proper Cultivation. The Lands are Rich and fertile in the Interior part of the province and on the sides of the Reviers which are numerous, Fruits and Grain may be raised with little labor. The late Inhabitants had often two crops of Indian corn in the same year and the Breeder here will be under no necessity of laying Fodder for the Winter corn for there is at all time sufficient quantity of pasture to maintain Cattle.*
>
> *Governor James Grant, 1772*

Fruits

Oranges

The firm of Panton, Leslie & Company established productive trading in St. Augustine. Settlers as well as Seminole Indians could order supplies from Europe and the English colonies which were unavailable in Florida.

Mary Peavett's Orange Toast

2 oranges, sectioned
8 slices hard bread
1/2 c light corn syrup
4 eggs, beaten
1/4 c honey
1 c buttermilk
3 T orange juice
1/2 t salt
1/8 t ginger, ground
2 T olive oil
1/4 t cinnamon
1/2 c orange marmalade

In a small pan combine syrup, honey, juice, and ginger. Heat to boiling. Add orange sections. Set aside. In shallow dish, add eggs. Stir in buttermilk, salt, and cinnamon. In a large skillet, heat oil. Dip bread in egg mixture, coating both sides. Cook 2-3 slices at a time for 1-2 minutes per side or until golden brown. Top with warm orange marmalade. Yields 4-8 servings.

Florida Fruit Casserole

The persimmon, an orange-red fruit, is edible only when completely ripe.

1 c pears, sliced
1 c apples, cored, sliced
1 c peaches, sliced
1 c persimmons, seeded, sliced
1 c oranges, sectioned
1 c grapefruit, sectioned
1 c sherry
2 T flour
1/4 c butter

Place fruit in a casserole dish. In saucepan heat butter, add flour and sherry, then stir. Pour mixture over fruit. Bake at 300° for 30 minutes. Yields 6-8 servings.

Apples

Baked English Mincemeat Apples

apples, hard baking type
rum
mincemeat
1/4 c butter, melted

Carefully cut off tops of apples and scoop out core. Do not cut through the bottom. Moisten mincemeat with rum and stuff into apples. Dribble butter on each apple and bake at 350° for 1 hour or until done. Baste occasionally. Yields however many apples you bake.

Hot Rum Valencia

3 c Valencia oranges, sectioned
1/4 c butter
2 T rum
3/4 c dark brown sugar
2 T cinnamon

Place orange sections in casserole. In saucepan heat butter, sugar, and rum. Pour over fruit and bake at 350° for 30 minutes. Sprinkle with cinnamon. Yields 4-6 servings.

African slaves contributed to the economy in St. Augustine. The success of the plantation system introduced into Florida by the English relied almost completely on servitude. Since available labor was not a factor, the British did not want for food as had the Spanish. Indeed, their plantations were as productive as the plantations in the other English colonies.

Vegetables

Boiled Cabbage

1 head cabbage, quartered
1 T olive oil
1 T cream
1 T vinegar
salt and pepper to taste
1/2 lb salted bacon, diced
1 red pepper pod
6 c water
1/2 c salt

Place cabbage and salt in pot and cover with 4 c water for several hours. In kettle add 2 c water, vinegar, bacon, and pepper pod and bring to a boil. Add cabbage and remaining ingredients and boil 15 minutes. Drain, fine chop all vegetables then add cream and reheat. Yields 4 servings.

Grant's Villa Cabbage Pudding

1 head cabbage, quartered
1/2 lb salted bacon, diced
2 T olive oil
1 c milk
3 eggs, lightly beaten
2 t dried mustard
salt and pepper to taste
l c bread crumbs
2 c water

Boil cabbage and bacon in water for 30 minutes. When thoroughly done, drain and chop fine. Add oil, milk, eggs, and seasonings. Pour into buttered deep dish and top with bread crumbs. Bake 30 minutes at 325° or until light brown. Yields 4 servings.

Datil Pepper

Minorcan Pickled Mushrooms

1 c mushrooms, halved
1/4 t pepper
1 T datil pepper
1 bay leaf
1/2 c red wine vinegar
1 clove garlic, minced
1 onion, thinly sliced
1 t salt

Layer mushrooms and onions in a quart jar. Boil remaining ingredients for several minutes. Pour into glass container. Yields 3 cups.

Minorcan
Datil Pepper-Cheese Pie

12 slices bacon, crisp, crumbled
1/2 c feta cheese, crumbled
1/4 c green onions, sliced
3/4 c flour, self-rising
1/3 c red bell peppers, cored, chopped
1 c milk
1 T basil
3 eggs
2 T datil peppers, seeded, minced

Mix bacon, onions, and peppers, and pour into a greased pie pan. Sprinkle with cheese. Combine remaining ingredients and stir. Pour on top. Bake 30-35 minutes at 350° or until knife inserted in center comes out clean. Cool for 5 minutes. Yields 6 servings.

Carrots Marinade

1 lb carrots, thinly sliced
salt and pepper to taste
1 c white wine
2 t sugar
1 c water
2 t lemon juice
1 clove garlic, minced
1/8 t parsley
1/8 t thyme
1/8 t tarragon
12 black olives, pitted
5 T olive oil

In a saucepan combine all ingredients except carrots, parsley, and black olives. Bring to a boil and simmer for 10 minutes. Add carrots and boil until tender, but still crisp. Cool then add black olives and parsley. Yields 4-6 servings.

English Peas and Corn

2 c English peas
2 c corn
1 c green onions, chopped
1/2 t thyme
1/2 t parsley
1 T pepper
1 t salt
1/2 c olive oil
1 c cream, soured
1 c water

Place vegetables, except onions, in pot with water, cover, and steam until tender. Drain. In skillet add oil and seasonings then brown onions. Add vegetables to skillet and stir once. Add cream, stir gently then heat, but do not boil. Yields 4 servings.

Bella Vista Vegetable Garden

Sauce:
3 T olive oil
1 c feta cheese, crumbled
3 T flour
1 c milk

Casserole:
1 c English peas
1 c lima beans
1 c corn
1 bell pepper, cored, chopped
1 T rum
1 T chili sauce
1 c cream
1-1/2 c feta cheese, crumbled
6 eggs, hard boiled, chopped
1/4 c olive oil
3 slices bread, toasted, crumbled

Sauce: In saucepan heat oil then stir in flour. Add milk and cheese, stirring constantly. Set aside.

Casserole: Simmer vegetables in oil until tender. Add cream, rum, chili sauce, and cheese. Stir constantly until cheese melts. Place in a 2 quart casserole and cover with cheese sauce then bread crumbs. Dot with egg and oil. Bake at 325° for 30-35 minutes or until brown. Yields 4-6 servings.

Governor Moore's Rice Dressing

2 c rice
1 T basil
2 c beef broth
1 T thyme
1 c onions, chopped
1/2 c bell peppers, cored, chopped
1/4 c parsley
1/4 c olive oil
1/4 t paprika
2 c water

Brown vegetables in oil. Add remaining ingredients and bring to a quick boil, then reduce heat and simmer 30-45 minutes. Yields 4-6 servings.

St. Francis Barracks' Onions and Potatoes

6 med potatoes, cubed
2 med onions, chopped
1 c yellow cheese, grated
1 egg, beaten
salt and pepper to taste
2 c water
olive oil

In pan combine potatoes, water, salt, and pepper. Cook over medium heat until tender. Pour off juice and save. Mash potatoes. Add egg, cheese, and onions, and mix well. Place in greased casserole and pour a little of the re-

served juice over all. Sprinkle additional cheese on top. Bake at 350° approximately 30 minutes. Yields 4-6 servings.

By the 1770s the seeds of revolution were sprouting throughout Colonial America, everywhere that is, except in Colonial Florida. British subjects there remained loyal to the Crown an action which eventually caused them great discomfort. American patriots from Georgia crossed the St. Mary's River into East Florida, plundering farms, burning crops, looting, and aggravating the British.

Turbulent times continued for a decade. But even as the American Revolution swept to its zenith, John Moultrie reported that his plantation, Bella Vista, was more productive than ever.

> *... plows and carts going in the fields ... more rice than I can beat out .... Fine stock of cattle and hogs and plenty of beef, fish, butter and cream cheese.*
> John Moultrie, 1778

Sweets

John Moultrie's Cream Cheese Delight

Cake:
40 oz cream cheese, softened
1-1/4 c sweet cracker crumbs
3 T flour
1 lemon rind, grated
1/2 orange rind, grated
1-3/4 c sugar
5 eggs

1/4 c butter, melted
1/4 c sugar
2 egg yolks
1/4 c heavy whipping cream

Fruit:
1/2 c orange sections
1/2 c grapefruit sections
sliced figs
1/4 c grapes, seedless, halved

Glaze:
1 T lemon juice
1 T flour
3/4 c water
1/4 c sugar
2 T cold water

Cake: Mix cracker crumbs, 1/4 c sugar, and butter. Grease a 10" springform pan and press crumb mixture onto bottom and sides of pan. Beat cream cheese until fluffy. Mix 1-3/4 c sugar and flour and gradually blend into cheese. Add rinds. Add eggs and egg yolks one at a time, beating well after each. Stir in cream. Turn into crust. Bake at 400° for 10 minutes. Reduce heat to 200° and bake 1 hour longer. Remove from oven and place away from drafts. Let cool then remove sides of pan and put cake on serving plate.

Fruit: Arrange fruit on cooled cake, 4-5 orange sections around center, surrounded by a circle of grapefruit sections, and a border of sliced figs and grapes.

Glaze: Combine 3/4 c water, sugar, and lemon juice. In separate bowl, combine cornstarch with 2 T cold water. Add to juices and cook until thick, stirring constantly. Spoon over fruit. Yields 10-12 servings.

King George's Gingerbread

1 c molasses
1/2 t soda
1/2 c sugar
1 c water, boiling
1/2 c olive oil
2-1/2 c flour, sifted
2 t ginger
2 eggs, well beaten
2 t cloves
powdered sugar

In bowl combine molasses, sugar, oil, ginger, and cloves. Dissolve soda in boiling water and stir into mixture. Then add flour and eggs. Stir well. Batter will be very thin. Fill greased and floured baking pan 3/4 full. Bake 30 minutes at 375°. Sprinkle with powdered sugar. Yields 12 servings.

British Wild Jelly Cookies

Blossom extract:
4 c water
4 c blossoms (violets, dandelion, clover, rose)

Jelly:
4 c blossom extract
1 T lemon juice
1/2 c pectin
5 c sugar

Cookie Batter:
1 c butter, softened
1 egg
1/2 c brown sugar, packed
2-1/2 c flour

Extract: Boil water and pour over blossoms. Let sit overnight. The following day strain blossoms. Reserve liquid for jelly.

Jelly: Combine extract, lemon juice, and pectin. Bring to a full boil. Add sugar and bring to a second boil, stirring constantly so sugar will not stick to bottom of pan. Boil one minute then skim foam from surface. Allow to cool before adding to cookie mixture.

Batter: Cream together butter, sugar, and egg. Slowly add flour and mix well. Form dough into small balls about 1" in diameter. Place on cookie sheet and make indentation with your thumb. Fill with jelly. Bake at 350° for 12-15 minutes until lightly browned. Yields approximately 2 dozen.

Mulberry Rum Balls

1 c mulberry nuts, finely chopped
2-1/2 c crackers, crushed
2 T unsweetened chocolate, grated
3 T white corn syrup
1 c powdered sugar
1/4 c rum
1/2 c powdered sugar, sifted

Mix crackers, chocolate, 1 c sugar, and nuts. Add corn syrup and rum. Blend well. Form into 1" balls then roll each in sifted sugar. Yields approximately 3 dozen.

Fort St. Marks Potato Pudding

4 med potatoes, peeled, grated
1 c persimmon, seedless, mashed
4 eggs, separated
3/4 c milk
1/2 c butter, softened
1 c water
1-1/2 c sugar
1/8 t salt
1 c coconut, grated
1 t vanilla

Beat yolks with all ingredients except egg whites. Beat egg whites then fold into mixture. Pour into a greased baking dish and bake at 300° approximately 20-30 minutes until brown and solid. Yields 4-6 servings.

Over the Ocean Bread Pudding

10 slices bread
1/2 c butter, melted
1 c figs (or other fruit)
1/2 c brown sugar
4 eggs, beaten
1 c milk
1/2 t cinnamon

Place bread on bottom of large greased pan. Pour butter on top of bread then spread fruit over bread. Sprinkle with sugar. Beat eggs and milk and pour over mixture. Bake at 350° for 45 minutes to 1 hour. Sprinkle with cinnamon. Yields 5-10 servings.

Old English Rice Frumenty

1 c rice, cooked
1/2 c milk
2/3 c sugar
1/4 c water
salt and pepper to taste
2 T butter
3 eggs, beaten
1 T rum
1 T cinnamon

To rice add sugar, salt, and pepper and cook on medium heat for 10 minutes. Add milk and water, cooking an additional 5 minutes. Add butter and eggs and blend well. Add remaining ingredients, except cinnamon. Stir well and simmer 5 minutes.

Ximenez-Fatio House.
Detached kitchen with
British style fireplace and oven

Sprinkle with cinnamon. Yields 2-4 servings.

Orange Grove Pudding

2 c oranges, sectioned
3 eggs
1 c molasses
1/4 t cinnamon
2 T flour
1 c milk
1/2 c butter, melted

Mix all ingredients together. Bake in a greased baking dish at 350° for about 1 hour or until solid. Yields 4-6 servings.

As the years passed and the American Revolution continued, wealthy compatriots from the infidel colony in South Carolina were "imprisoned" in British St. Augustine. Included among those unfortunates were Edward Rutledge, Arthur Middleton, and Thomas Heyward, Jr.,

signers of the Declaration of Independence. They were brought from Charleston, South Carolina in 1780 when the city fell to the English. In St. Augustine "imprisonment" for those men meant that they were free to wander through the city during the daytime, but were expected to abide by a curfew at dusk. The men were granted permission to rent a house and to bring a slave with them from their plantation. The more "dangerous" rebels were held captive in Fort St. Marks, formerly the Castillo de San Marcos.

Breads

Loaf Bread

4 c flour
1 t salt
1 t sugar
1 c water
1/4 c butter
1 pkg prepared yeast

Mix ingredients together with the exception of 1-1/2 c flour. Set aside to rise. When risen work in remaining flour, adding a bit of water if needed. Work smoothly and set to rise again. When risen, add a small amount of oil, work in well, let stand an hour then put in a well greased bread pan and bake at 300° for about an hour. Yields 1 loaf.

Plantation Rice Bread

2 c milk
1 c rice, cooked
2 c cornmeal, sifted
1/2 c olive oil
3 eggs, beaten
1/2 t salt

Combine all ingredients. Beat well, then pour into a greased muffin mold. Bake at 400° for approximately 15-20 minutes or until brown. Yields 2 dozen.

Fort St. Marks Brown Bread

3/4 c sifted flour
3 T oil
1-1/4 t soda
1 c buttermilk
1 t salt
1 egg, beaten well
1 c bread, crumbled
1 c dates (or other fruit)

Sift flour, soda, and salt together. Mix in bread crumbs. Cut in oil until mixture resembles fine meal. Mix rest of ingredients and stir until well blended. Fill 2 greased bread pans half full. Bake 45-50 minutes at 375°. Let cool 10 minutes then turn upside down and tap on bottom of pan. Remove and let cool on wire rack. Yields 2 loaves.

Beverages

By the end of 1764 and Governor James Grant's first year in office, he and his guests had consumed vast quantities of alcohol that had been stored in the cellars of Government House. Meticulous records kept during his tenure recorded that they drank 86 gallons of Jamaican rum, 150 gallons of common rum, 140 gallons of Madeira wine, 76 gallons of Teneriff, 1,200 bottles of claret, 519 bottles of port, sweet wine, champagne, beer, and ale. No wonder Grant suffered from gout!

Yule Time Eggnog

12 eggs, divided
1/2 lb sugar
1 5th Jamaican rum
2 c milk
4 c heavy cream
cinnamon and cloves

Beat egg yolks until light. Stir in milk and rum. Pour into large bowl. Beat egg whites, cream, and sugar until stiff. Fold in. Dust with spices. Yields 20 servings.

Government House Rum Libation

3 parts dark Jamaican rum
1 part molasses
2 parts lemon juice

Combine ingredients and shake vigorously. Yields whatever you prepared.

Madeira Wine Punch

1 gal Madeira wine
1 qt white wine
1 qt gin
8 c water

Mix well. Yields 12-20 servings.

His Majesty's Spiced Tea

1 c orange juice
1 stick cinnamon
6 T lemon juice
12 cloves
4 c water
1-3/4 c sugar
4 t tea leaves
2 c Jamaican rum

Boil cloves and cinnamon for 20 minutes in 2 c water. Remove spices and set pot aside. In another pot boil tea in 2 c water, strain, then add to first pot. Stir in fruit juices, rum, and sugar. Yields 9 servings.

Legend has it that the storeroom in Mary Peavett's oldest house painted red to warn of "danger," possibly because the room was used for fermenting beer. Stored in large wooden casks, the golden brew was known to ex-

plode on occasion, creating danger for all those nearby. Fact or fancy, at the time red was a popular color for decorating rooms.

Mary's Ginger Beer

1-1/2 oz ginger
1-1/2 oz cream of tartar
1 lb brown sugar
2 lemons, thinly sliced
1/2 pt yeast
8 c water

Boil water then add all ingredients. Let stand, covered, for 2 weeks. Yields 20 servings.

Hard times befell the British after two successful decades in Florida. In 1781 the Spanish, taking advantage of the war between America and England, captured Pensacola, West Florida's capital. Several months later Britain's Lord Cornwallis surrendered to General George Washington at Yorktown, Virginia. By 1783 British refugees were pouring into East Florida. St. Augustine's population at that time was approaching 2,000 whites and 3,000 Negro slaves. Over the next several months, the number drastically increased as an additional 8,300 Negro slaves and 5,000 whites fled from Carolina and Georgia across the St. Mary's River into East Florida.

With such an alarming influx of refugees, food shortages, unknown throughout the British occupation, again cast a shadow over St. Augustine. Once agriculturally productive, this English colony could no longer feed its population. Chaos was at hand.

Then, to make matters worse, at the conclusion of the American Revolution, the 1783 Treaty of Paris returned Florida to Spain. British colonists were notified they had two choices: Evacuate or remain.

Kitchen at the Spanish Barracks

Chapter IV.
The Spanish Return
1784-1821

The Spanish flag rose again over impressive Castillo de San Marcos as British St. Augustine was renamed Spanish San Agustín. The exodus of yet another group of settlers began as they abandoned their homes, their gardens, and their livestock. The Minorcans, unable to afford passage home and now rooted in San Agustín, remained. Appointed governor of *La Florida* was Vicente de Zéspedes from Havana, Cuba. He sailed to his new position accompanied by hundreds of soldiers and their families. Crossing the bar into Matanzas Bay, these new settlers, combined with those who remained in San Agustín, brought the mixed population of the military outpost to approximately 1,700, including Minorcans, French, Germans, Swiss, Greeks, Italians, 300 English, Scots, Irish, and Americans. And it was the new governor who had the ominous responsibility to provide flour, salt meat, and produce for his colony.

Although food was often scarce during the Second Spanish Period for the common folk, the Governor evidently had no trouble providing for himself and his guests. When the United States Revolutionary War General Nathaniel Greene visited San Agustín in 1785, he was entertained quite lavishly. Writing home to his wife, he remarked that:

> *I believe in my soul there was from one hundred and fifty to two hundred dishes of different kinds served up in seven courses.*
>
> General Nathaniel Greene, 1785

Since class distinction was judged according to the number of courses served at a meal, General Greene could not have missed the message he was presented by Governor Zéspedes.

Possibly the chefs at Government House had access to two popular cookbooks of the period when they created such an array of courses:

> *Take the hardboiled eggs and peel them. Put them in a pot with seasoned water. Fry plenty of onion and add parsley, mint and other herbs and a hazelnut sauce, and bring to boil. Then add some bread soaked in water and vinegar. Crush some hazelnuts with two cloves of garlic, and add oil with fried garlic to the eggs. Thin the sauce with the seasoned water: the quantity of sauce depends on the number of eggs.*
>
> Juan de la Mata, Nuevo Arte de Cocina, 1745

> *The most common Gazpacho is known as the Capon de Galera, which is made as follows: take the crusts of a one-pound loaf of bread, without the crumbs, toast them and soak in water: afterwards put them in their Sauce, composed of anchovy bones, and a couple of cloves of Garlic, well ground, with vinegar, sugar, Salt and Oil, all thoroughly mixed, letting the bread soften in the garlic. Then put it all on the plate, adding all or some of the ingredients and vegetables of the Royal Salad.*
>
> *Juan de la Mata, Arte de Reposteria, 1747*

The gazpacho, introduced to Spain by the Arabs, was a popular form of soup. Ingredients were added in a specific order to a mortar and pestle, ground then stirred into a thick substance—bread, water, oil, salt, vinegar garlic—then whatever else the cook desired to include. Herb gardens from British days added new spices for the Spanish.

While the Governor and his family and guests dined with gusto, the townspeople gathered in the Plaza de Armas just beyond the windows of Government House to barter and sell their meager produce. Most Minorcans excelled in fishing, so fish was always plentiful. Families, such as the Genopolys, rented land from the government north of the fort to raise and sell produce. Market days brought to the center of town a rich assortment of shoppers, strollers, and vendors including the Seminole Indians. Dressed in loincloths and blankets and smelling of bear grease for their hair, the Indians hawked fresh venison and hog, wild honey and bees wax. But before returning to their villages, the Seminoles would often purchase a bottle of rum or aguardiente de caña and sleep their adventures off under the trees, the stars, or the Spanish balconies.

The Spanish during this period continued their eating traditions as they had during the First Spanish Period. But because there remained so many other nationalities, the flavor and cuisine of old San Agustín was becoming cosmopolitan. By now the versatile and popular tomato appeared on the list of staples in town. The tomato had originated in South America and was domesticated by the

Marketing at the Plaza de Armas

Kitchen area of the Oldest House

In 1790, Gerónimo Alvarez bought the Peavett's house, now known as the Oldest House, through public auction. Soon after, the British fireplace was sealed and a detached kitchen was built toward the back of the property to reduce heat during the intense San Agustín summers.

A detached kitchen was also practical for reducing the threat of a house fire. Since shelves and cupboards were still not used in the colony, dishes were washed after a meal and the dining table was reset to await the next meal.

Incas of Peru who bred the fruit so it would have many ruffles and ridges. When the Spanish conquistadores invaded Incan cities, they took the tomato seeds back to Spain where Spanish monks cultivated them. Fearful of "exotic" plants indigenous to the New World, much of Europe did not accept the tomato, as well as the potato or bell pepper, as edible food sources for several hundred years. Along with the tomato, celery, a long-time Mediterranean food, added texture and flavor to San Agustín cuisine.

Since the Spanish did not like indoor English fireplaces, they constructed kitchens with baking ovens at the back of their property or continued to use the practical fogón.

English cooking utensils had been left behind and many more were imported, especially for use by the upper class. As far as eating utensils, there were changes in design and production. Pottery continued to be imported from Spain or Mexico. Most preservation and storage methods remained as they had during the British occupation. Ice was still unknown in La Florida.

Tinaja for storing food

A Spanish and Minorcan favorite was the "pisto" or vegetable stew mixture made of tomatoes, bell peppers, and a variety of other vegetables. Since the datil pepper was the most prominent spice used by the Minorcans, datil pepper sauce added a memorable flavor to Hispanic cuisine.

San Agustín
Datil Pepper Sauce

2 c tomatoes, crushed
1 c datil peppers, chopped
1 c figs, crushed
2 c red wine vinegar
2 T chili powder
1 T cumin
1 T basil
1/2 t salt
1 t pepper
1 T brown sugar
1 T olive oil

Combine all ingredients and beat well. Pour into kettle, bring to a rapid boil, then reduce heat and simmer for 2 hours. Seal in jars. Yields approximately 2 quarts.

Mayor, Carne, y Ave

Game, Meat, and Fowl

Hamburguesas de Puerco
Pork Patties

2 lbs pork, ground
1/4 c olive oil
4 onions, diced
2 cloves garlic, minced
2 T datil pepper sauce
2 t basil
1 T pepper
1 t salt
2 c bread crumbs
4 T flour

Combine meat and seasonings and shape into patties. Sift flour over each then brown in oil. Combine remaining ingredients in saucepan and cook 30 minutes. When meat is done add sauce and then heat an additional 5 minutes. Yields 2-4 servings.

Picadillo Sopa
Spicy Beef Soup

1 lb pork or beef, ground
2 onions, diced
1 c tomatoes, crushed
3 cloves garlic, minced
2 T datil pepper sauce
1/2 c Spanish olives, thinly sliced
1/2 c bell pepper, cored, diced
1 c rice
2 c water
1/4 c olive oil
2 t salt
1 t sugar

Place meat in a large kettle and brown in oil. Remove meat and brown onions, bell pepper, and garlic. Add remaining ingredients, stir well. Add meat and water. Simmer, covered, for 30 minutes. Yields 6-8 servings.

Estofado de Tortuga Ardillon
Gopher Turtle Stew

Since the Florida gopher turtle is listed by the federal government as a species of special concern, beef or pork should be substituted.

4 gopher turtles
20 c water
6 onions, diced
4 T datil pepper sauce
6 potatoes, cubed
3 cloves garlic, crushed
1 bay leaf
1 T salt

1 T pepper
1/2 lb salt bacon, thinly sliced
1/2 c flour
1 c red wine
2 c water
3 c tomatoes, crushed
1/2 c olive oil

In a large pot bring water to a boil. Drop in gopher turtles, one at a time and cook 5 minutes then remove. Discard water and cut meat from gophers, including neck, legs, and claw. Discard remainder of turtles. Combine salt, pepper, and flour, and dredge meat. In same pot fry bacon, garlic, and onion in oil until brown. Add all ingredients to pot and bring to a quick boil. Reduce heat and simmer, covered, for 1 hour or until meat is tender. Yields 6-8 servings.

In 1773, William Bartram, a famous naturalist from Pennsylvania, traveled extensively throughout Florida, Georgia, and Alabama. After wandering for three years through the south, chronicling his impressions and experiences, and cataloging in great detail the plant and animal kingdom, his book, Travels, *was published. As Bartram often wrote, in Florida he found his paradise.*

> *I accordingly proceeded and made good my entrance into the lagoon, though not without opposition from the alligators, who formed a line across the entrance, but did not pursue me into it, nor was I molested by any there, though there were some very large ones in a cove.*
> *William Bartram, 1791*

Caimán a la Parilla
Grilled Alligator Tail

4 alligator tail steaks, sliced 1" thick
salt and pepper to taste
2 T olive oil
2 cloves garlic, minced
1 T paprika
2 T datil peppers, crushed

Brown garlic in oil then add seasonings. Place alligator steaks on grill 3" from red hot coals. Baste with garlic sauce. Grill 3-4 minutes on each side basting at each turn until meat is tender. Yields 4 servings.

Quail

Codorniz y Ostras
Quail and Oysters

6 quail, dressed
1/2 lb oysters
1 bunch green onions, chopped
3 T olive oil
6 slices bacon
salt and pepper to taste

Wrap one slice bacon around each quail. Arrange in oiled baking dish. Season with salt and pepper. Cover dish and bake at 325° for 45 minutes. Brown oysters and onions in oil then add to quail and bake 15 minutes longer. Yields 6 servings.

Higados de Pollo Con Vino
Chicken Livers in Wine

4 lbs chicken livers
6 onions, diced
4 T flour
1/2 c olive oil
1 t salt
2 T datil pepper sauce
1 t pepper
2 c chicken broth
1 c white wine
8 c rice, cooked

Heat oil in large pot and add livers, onions, and spices. Stir until brown then stir in flour. Add wine and broth, cover, and simmer 30 minutes. Serve over rice. Yields 8 servings.

As with the First Spanish Period, food continued to be scarce throughout most of the Second Spanish Period. However, by the end of the 1790s, poultry, swine, and beef became more plentiful.

Cattle ranches were raising the gangly descendant of the first cattle brought from Spain, the Andalusian. Produce from small farms supplied a variety of vegetables including squash, melons, yams, sweet peppers, chayote, and tomatoes. Groves were plentiful with grapes, peaches, bananas, citrus, dates, and figs.

Banana Stalk

The Minorcans bartered fresh fish for vegetables, fruit, and meat, as well as fishing nets which they expertly wove.

Pescado y Marisco

Fish and Seafood

Governor Zéspedes distributed land lying beyond the city's boundaries for cattle grazing and cultivation. Some of the Minorcan families, who by now numbered almost 500, accepted this offer. They and their few slaves moved to the northwest section where many of their descendants reside today. The Minorcans farmed the soil, but their hearts were not in agriculture for their souls belonged to the sea.

Having once lived on the island of Minorca, surrounded by the Mediterranean, salt water coursed through the veins of the Minorcans. They brought with them to the New World their seafaring and fishing skills.

Pescado Rojo Cremoso
Creamed Red Fish

1 lb red fish, filleted
1/2 c olive oil
2 T flour
1 c milk
1 T pepper
2 slices hard bread, toasted

Soak fish overnight to freshen. Boil 10 minutes then drain water and flake fish. In a saucepan combine remaining ingredients except bread. Stir until blended. Add fish, stir, then pour over bread. Yields 2 servings.

"Drum" Horneado
Baked Drum

2 lbs drum
1 T salt
1 T pepper
1/4 lb salt pork, diced
1 lg onion, chopped
8 potatoes, peeled, sliced
2 T datil pepper, crushed
1 c water

Place fish in a large baking pan, sprinkle with salt and peppers. Fry salt pork and onions until brown then place mixture over fish. Lay potatoes over mixture and cover with water. Bake at 325° for 45 minutes. Yields 4 servings.

"Mullet" Frito
Fried Mullet

The popular cry "mullet on the beach" proclaimed to the Minorcans that their favorite fish was in numerous supply along the shoreline.

1 mullet
1 t salt
1 t pepper
1/2 c cornmeal
1/2 c olive oil

Cut off tail and head of mullet and split down the middle. Remove the back bone. Wash and dry. Sprinkle with salt, pepper, and cornmeal. Heat oil in pan and fry fish on both sides until brown. Yields 2 servings.

Camarón y Pimientos
Shrimp and Peppers

1 lb shrimp, peeled, chopped
4 red bell peppers, cored
1/2 t pepper
1/2 t chili pepper
1/2 t salt
1/2 c oil
2 c onions, chopped
1/2 c bread crumbs
1/2 c feta cheese, crumbled (feta is made from ewe or goat milk, preserved in brine)
1 c water

In pot add peppers and salt and boil 5 minutes. Drain. Place shrimp, vegetables, except peppers, and seasonings in bowl and mix well. Heat oil in a large pot and add the mixture. Cook 6 minutes on medium heat stirring occasionally to keep mixture from sticking. Remove from heat and cool. Stuff mixture in peppers and place in greased baking dish. Cover peppers with bread crumbs and cheese. Bake at 350° for 30 minutes or until lightly browned. Yields 2-4 servings.

Cangrejo Estofado
Stewed Crabs

1 doz crabs, softshell
4 potatoes, peeled, quartered
1 onion, thinly sliced
2 T flour
salt and pepper to taste
1/2 c salt pork, diced
8 c water

Fry salt pork in a very large pot until brown. Combine remaining ingredients, cover, and simmer 1 hour. Yields 4 servings.

Estofado de Almejas Picante
Clam Chowder Datil Style

8 c clams, diced
1 lb salt pork, thinly sliced
3 c tomatoes, crushed
2 red peppers, cored, diced
1 T thyme
2 cloves garlic, crushed
4 onions, diced
4 T datil pepper
3 c water

In large pot cook pork until brown. Add onions, garlic, and red peppers, and continue cooking until brown. Add all seasonings and stir. Add tomatoes then bring mixture to a quick boil. Reduce heat, stirring periodically, then cover and simmer for 30 minutes. Add water and clams, bring back to a quick boil, then reduce heat and cook, stirring constantly, until clams are done, approximately 15 minutes. Yields 4 servings.

Camarón Frito de Abuelita
Granny Mac's Fried Shrimp

1 lb lg shrimp, shelled, deveined (leave tail on)
1 c flour
1 t salt
1/2 t baking powder
1/2 t paprika
1/2 t pepper
1/2 c oil
1 lemon, thinly sliced
water

Make a deep cut into the top of the shrimp to fan. Place in large bowl, cover with water and lemon.

Sift dry ingredients into a bowl. Dredge shrimp individually in mixture, coating thoroughly. When all are dredged, set aside. (Today's cooks discovered that chilling shrimp 30 minutes sets a better texture.) Heat oil until very hot. Drop shrimp, a few at a time, into oil and watch carefully. Too many shrimp at a time lowers the temperature of the oil and makes the shrimp soggy. Fry until golden, 3 minutes or so. Yields 2 servings.

Camarón Pilaf Estilo Minorca
Minorcan Shrimp Pilau

1 lb lg shrimp, shelled, deveined
4 c chicken broth
2 c rice, well washed
2 strips bacon, chopped
1/2 c onion, chopped
1/2 c celery, chopped
1 clove garlic, chopped
1 T pimento
1 T datil pepper sauce
1/4 c vinegar
salt, pepper, celery salt to taste

Brown bacon in heavy skillet. Then brown onions and celery in drippings. Add spices. Set aside and add pimento. Place chicken broth in large kettle and heat to boiling. Add salt, vinegar, and rice. Cover and reduce to simmer for 25 minutes. Immediately add drippings mixture and shrimp. Cover and let steam for 7-10 minutes. When shrimp are pink, they are done. Stir mixture thoroughly and add hot sauce to taste. Yields 6-8 servings.

Paella

Paella, the national dish of Spain, is also the name given the metal pan in which the food is prepared. Brought to Spain by the Romans, the pan is 2-3" deep, round, with two or more handles attached.

Traditionally, paella was positioned so that those eating it could sit in a circle with the food in the middle. Everyone had an individual utensil for eating and would section off a portion.

1 lb mussels, in shell
1 lb scallops, shelled, whole
2 lbs shrimp, cooked, shelled, diced
1 lb sausage, cooked, thinly sliced
1 lb clams, in shell
1/2 lb chicken, cooked, cubed
1 red pepper, diced
2 c yellow rice, cooked
2 c tomatoes, cubed
1 c bell pepper, diced
1 t salt
1/2 t cayenne pepper
4 c chicken broth
1 lg onion, diced
1/2 c black olives, pits removed
1/4 c pimentos
3 cloves garlic, minced
1 c green peas, cooked
1/4 c olive oil

In large pot cook onion and garlic in oil until translucent. Reduce heat and add remaining ingredients except seafood, meats, rice, peas, and olives. Simmer several minutes, stirring occasionally. Add sausage and chicken and simmer 5 minutes. Add seafood and rice, cover, and simmer 10 minutes. Stir in peas and olives. Yields 8 servings.

A favorite Sunday pastime of the Spanish and the Minorcans was a convité, or picnic, often held at the site of old Fort Mose. Bushels of oysters from the North River were retrieved from its shallow waters. A roaring fire was built, and after it was reduced to hot coals, the oysters were banked alongside the coal pit and covered with a heavy wet cloth. After an hour or so the oysters were ready to shuck and then dip into the Minorcans' famous datil pepper sauce.

Frutas y Verduras

Fruits and Vegetables

While many townspeople maintained small gardens in their yards, more and more families moved beyond the city limits. They rented land from the government and raised corn, beans, potatoes, lentils, squash, pumpkin, rice, and fruit trees.

> It now being almost night, I returned to my camp, where I had . . . excellent oranges hanging in abundance over my head (a valuable substitute for vinegar). I sat down and reglaed myself cheerfully.
> William Bartram, 1791

Ensalada de Naranja de Florida
Florida Orange Salad

8 oranges, sectioned
4 egg yolks, beaten
1 T sugar
1/4 c vinegar
1/4 t salt
1 T olive oil
1/2 c cream

Cook all ingredients, except oranges and cream, stirring constantly, until thick. Remove from heat and cool. Add cream. Gently stir in orange sections. Yields 6-8 servings.

Peras Horneadas
Baked Pears

8 pears, cored, sliced
1 T lemon juice
1/2 c honey
1/4 c water
1/2 c molasses
1 t ginger
1 T cinnamon
1 t mace
1 t nutmeg

Place pears in large baking dish. Mix all ingredients and pour over pears. Bake at 325° for 15-20 minutes. Yields 8 servings.

Sopa de Frijol Negro
Black Bean Soup

1 lb black beans, soaked overnight
1 t salt
2 cloves garlic, minced
1/4 c oil
1 c onion, diced
1 c bell pepper, cored, diced
1 T pepper
1/4 t sage
2 T vinegar
1 bay leaf
8 c water

In a large kettle, brown onion, bell pepper, and spices in oil. Add remaining ingredients. Simmer 4-6 hours or until beans are tender. Yields 6 servings.

Sopa de Lentejas
Lentil Soup

1 lb lentils
1 ham hock
2 onions, chopped
1/4 c oil
2 T vinegar
2 t salt
1 clove garlic, minced
2 stalks celery, thinly sliced
1 c chicken broth
4 c water

Simmer lentils in water 1 hour. In oil brown onion, garlic, and celery then add to lentils. Add remaining ingredients and simmer 1 hour or until lentils are tender. Yields 6-8 servings.

Sopa de Calabaza
Pumpkin Soup

1 lg pumpkin, peeled, diced
3 c water
4 t salt
1/4 c butter
2 t cinnamon
2 T brown sugar
3 c cream
3 c water
cinnamon for garnish

Place pumpkin in large pot with salt and 3 c water. Bring to a boil and cook until pumpkin is soft, approximately 15 minutes. Drain liquid. Mash pumpkin, then add seasonings. Simmer 15 minutes, stirring occasionally. Slowly add 3 c water and cream and continue stirring until well blended. Simmer another 10 minutes. Sprinkle with cinnamon. Yields 6-8 servings.

Sopa de Garbanzo
Spanish Bean Soup

1 lb garbanzo, soaked overnight
1 lb chorizo sausage, thinly sliced
4 med potatoes, diced
1/2 lb salt pork, diced

1 T pepper
2 t saffron
8 c water

Drain beans, rinse, and put back in large kettle. Add water and spices. In skillet fry salt pork and onions until brown. Drain then add to kettle. Simmer for 2 hours. Add potatoes and sausage and simmer 45 minutes. Yields 6-8 servings.

Pimientos Fritos
Fried Peppers

4 lg bell peppers, cored, sliced
1 clove garlic, crushed
3 T olive oil
1 t salt
1 T datil pepper sauce

Brown garlic in oil. Add remaining ingredients and stir briskly over high heat. Reduce heat, cover, and simmer for 15 minutes. Serves 4.

Pimientos de Avilés
Peppers Avilés

2 lg onions, chopped
3 T green chili peppers, chopped
1 clove garlic, minced
1 lb feta cheese, crumbled
1/4 c olive oil
6 tomatoes, crushed
2 T datil pepper sauce
1 T flour
6 slices hard bread

Brown onions and garlic in oil. Add peppers and datil sauce. Reduce heat then add cheese and melt. Add tomatoes. Stir. Add flour, stirring until thick. Pour over slices of hard bread. Yields 6 servings.

San Juan Calabaza con Naranja
St. Johns Squash with Orange

1 squash, thickly cut
1 T lemon juice
1/4 c butter
2 T honey
1 t ginger
2 T orange juice
1 T orange rind, grated
olive oil

Arrange squash in bottom of an oiled baking dish. In a small saucepan, heat butter, honey, and juices, stirring until well blended. Pour over squash. Sprinkle with spices and rind then bake at 350° for 45 minutes. Yields 2 servings.

Cazuela de Calabaza
Squash Casserole

3 c squash, cooked, mashed
1 sm onion, chopped
2 eggs, beaten
1/2 t salt
1 c crackers, crushed
1-1/2 c yellow cheese, grated
1/2 c milk
1 T sugar
1 T butter
1 T pepper
1/2 c hickory nuts, chopped
1 T olive oil

Combine squash, sugar, salt, oil, and onion. Stir well. Add milk, eggs, cheese, crackers, and pepper. Mix well then pour into a greased baking dish. Sprinkle with nuts and butter. Bake at 325° for 30 minutes. Yields 4-6 servings.

Cazuela de Berenjena
Eggplant Casserole

1 lg eggplant, peeled, cubed
1/4 c olive oil
1 bell pepper, cored, diced
2 T brown sugar
1 lg onion, diced
1 T pepper
1/2 t salt
2 c tomatoes, crushed
1/2 c yellow cheese, grated
1/2 c bread crumbs

Brown pepper, onion, and eggplant in oil. Add remaining ingredients, except cheese and bread. Simmer until mixture thickens, stirring occasionally. Pour into well-greased baking dish, top with cheese and bread crumbs. Bake at 325° for 45 minutes. Yields 6 servings.

Cazuela de Elote
Corn Casserole

2 c corn
1/4 c olive oil
2 T flour
1 t basil
1/4 c onion, minced
1/2 c bread crumbs
2 c tomatoes, crushed
1/2 c mushrooms, sliced
1 T datil pepper, minced

Heat oil then add flour and stir. Add remaining ingredients except bread crumbs and stir well. Pour into greased baking dish, cover mixture with bread crumbs, and bake at 350° for 30 minutes. Yields 4-6 servings.

Ensalada de Pimientos Rojas y Verdes
Red and Green Pepper Salad

3 red bell peppers, cored, thinly sliced
3 green bell peppers, cored, thinly sliced
3 onions, thinly sliced
1/2 c olive oil
1/2 c lemon juice
1 t salt
1 T pepper
1 T datil pepper sauce
2 cloves garlic, minced

Combine all ingredients in large bowl. Mix well. Yields 6-8 servings.

Tomates Estilo Minorca
Minorcan Tomatoes

2 c tomatoes, diced
1/2 c brown sugar
1/4 c datil pepper sauce
1 lg onion, diced
1/2 c bread crumbs
1/4 c olive oil

Brown onions in oil then add tomatoes and stir well. Add remaining ingredients except crumbs. Pour into a greased casserole dish, top with bread crumbs and bake at 325° for 1 hour. Yields 4-6 servings.

Dulces

Sweets

A Minorcan tradition introduced to San Agustín was the formatjada serenade. Young Minorcan men gathered in the public square on Easter Eve to form small groups of singers. These groups would then wander through the town serenad-

ing residents. The reward for such a songfest was a formatjada, a pastry of sugar, eggs, and various other rich ingredients.

Postre de Queso
Cheese Formatjadas

Filling:
6 eggs, well beaten
1 t nutmeg
1/2 t salt
1 lb sharp cheese, grated
1/2 t cayenne pepper

Pastry:
1-1/2 c butter, softened
1/4 c sugar
1/3 c flour
1 t salt
2 pkgs yeast
1/4 c water, warm
1 egg
1 c milk

Filling: Combine all ingredients and set aside.

Pastry: Dissolve yeast in warm water. In a large mixing bowl cream together butter, egg, flour, sugar, and salt. In saucepan scald milk, cool, then add to flour mixture. Add yeast and blend well. Let rest 30 minutes then knead several minutes and roll out on a well-floured board to 1/8" thick. Use a 4" round cookie cutter to cut circles. Spoon small portion of filling on one half of circle. Bring other half of dough over and pinch closed. Place on a greased pan and press ends of circles gently with fork. Using a sharp knife, make the sign of a cross in the top of each. Bake at 375° until golden. Yields approximately 1 dozen servings.

Mermelada de Higo
Fig Conserve

Fig Branch

2 lbs figs, sliced
1/2 t salt
1 c oranges, diced
1 c hickory nuts, chopped
2 med lemons, diced
1/2 c brown sugar

In saucepan combine figs, oranges, and lemons with sugar and salt. Bring to a boil and simmer until thick, but slightly runny. Stir in nuts. Store in sterile containers. Yields approximately 8 cups.

Pastel de Melaza
Molasses Cake

1-1/2 c flour, sifted
1-1/2 t baking soda
1 t cinnamon
1/4 t salt
1/2 t ginger
1/2 t nutmeg
1 egg, beaten
1/2 c butter, melted
1 c light molasses
1/2 c water, hot

Sift dry ingredients and set aside. In large bowl beat egg, butter, molasses, and water until well mixed. Add flour mixture and beat until smooth. Pour into a greased 9 x 9 x 1-3/4" pan and bake at 375° for 30-35 minutes. Yields 12 servings.

Pastel del Diablo
Devil's Food Cake

Cake:
2 c brown sugar
1/2 c cocoa
1/2 c butter, softened
1 c milk, soured
2 c flour
1 t vanilla
1 t soda
2 eggs

Icing:
3 T butter
3 oz chocolate square
5 T milk, heated
1-1/2 c powdered sugar, sifted
1/2 t vanilla
1/4 t salt

Cake: Combine all ingredients. Mix well and pour into two greased and floured cake pans. Bake at 350° for 30 minutes. Let cool.

Icing: Melt butter and chocolate in double boiler. Pour milk over sugar and stir until dissolved. Add vanilla, salt, and chocolate and beat until smooth and thick enough to spread over cake. Yields 12 servings.

Flan
Spanish Custard

Coating:
3/4 c sugar
1/4 c water

Custard:
5 eggs, well beaten
1 t vanilla
1/2 t salt

1 c sugar
2 c milk

Coating: Combine ingredients in small saucepan. Slow boil for 10-15 minutes until thick and brown. Pour into custard cups, carefully coating the sides.

Custard: Combine all ingredients in a bowl and mix well. Pour into custard cups. Place cups in a pan of hot water and bake at 350° until centers are firm. Yields 6-8 servings.

Tocino del Cielo
Egg Creme

1 c white sugar
1 c water
6 egg yolks
2 eggs

In saucepan simmer all but 1/4 c sugar in water for 8-10 minutes. Set aside to cool. Place remaining sugar in a flat metal mold. Heat until sugar hardens and turns brown. Set aside. In a bowl, combine eggs and beat well. Pour eggs into the sugar mixture and stir gently. Pour into the metal mold. Bake at 300° for 25-30 minutes. Yields 4 servings.

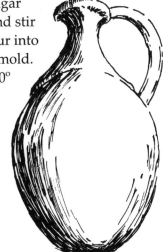

Storage container

Street Scene inside the City Gate

The Second Spanish Period was not a success for La Florida's founders. San Agustín's diverse population created a variety of problems for government officials.

Land speculators from the new country of America crossed the St. Mary's River in search of land. The once thriving cattle ranches of Northeast Florida had been raided by marauding bands of Indians and outlaws.

Slave owners from the former British colonies were demanding the return of their slaves. Pirates had begun to plunder La Florida's coast.

Then during the War of 1812, La Florida's western boundary shifted from the Mississippi to the Perdido River, substantially decreasing Spanish territory. In 1812, the American forces captured Pensacola, La Florida's western capital.

In 1817 and again in 1818, American forces reinvaded La Florida. Under the pretense of quelling what would become the First Seminole Indian War, the American government intentionally applied pressure on Spain in an attempt to acquire La Florida.

As always, for the Spanish at least, the sandy dry soil of the coastal region still refused to produce the quantity and quality of foods necessary for the welfare of the town. Indeed, La Florida had become increasingly difficult to govern. With continued international problems plaguing Spain, it finally relinquished its claim to La Florida after more than 200 years of occupation.

Chapter V.
The New American Territory
1821-1844

John Randolph, a member of the United States House of Representatives during the time the government was applying pressure on Spain to cede *La Florida* to America, was definitely *not* in favor of the acquisition. Outspoken and opinionated during the discussion, Randolph exploded from the house floor to argue that acquiring such an untamed land was ill-advised and useless.

> *Florida, sir, is not worth buying. It is a land of swamps, of quagmires, of frogs and alligators and mosquitoes! A man, sir, would not immigrate into Florida. No, sir! No man would immigrate into Florida — no, not from hell itself!*
>
> John Randolph, 1821

Obviously Randolph and his supporters did not share President James Monroe's vision. The President was convinced that to acquire *La Florida* would expand the emerging power of the United States in world politics; thus, he was more than willing for America to settle Spain's debts in return for *La Florida*. The investment: $5,000,000.

On July 10, 1821 the cannons of old Castillo de San Marcos boomed a final salute to the Spanish and a welcome to the Americans. The Spanish flag was lowered and the Stars and Stripes hoisted. And once again with the lowering of the Spanish flag, the sleepy hamlet of San Agustín became St. Augustine. The fort along the shore of the Matanzas was named Fort Marion in honor of General Francis Marion, the Revolutionary War hero from South Carolina. After almost two and a half centuries of Spanish occupation, San Agustín was still little more than a military outpost dependent on Cuba, Spain, and the English colonies. But although the Spanish colonists had relied on others, they had endured. And because they had remained loyal to *La Florida* for those many years, their little military outpost in 1821 was the oldest continually occupied city in the United States of America.

After the Americans took possession of Florida, few Spanish and British remained. The Minorcans stayed, as did the Africans, and a small number of French, Swiss, Greeks, Germans, Italians, and Seminole Indians. However, during this period of transition, fewer people lived in Florida than when Ponce de León set foot on its sandy soil in 1513.

After the Americans gained possession of La Florida, the land of abundant resources, numerous wild creatures began their descent toward extinction, including the black bear, all sea turtle species, a variety of migratory fowl, and the friendly sea cow or "manatee," the name the Spanish gave the massive creature which swam the warm waters of La Florida. Wild game was overhunted both as a sport as well as a food source.

Outdoor kitchens continued in use throughout the 19th century for safety measures as well as heat control. The early 1800s saw the invention of the wood-burning stove which replaced the old baking ovens and reduced the backbreaking bending and stirring in front of an open fireplace. These "woodeating" monsters, as they were nicknamed, became part of the American culinary landscape. Cooking habits changed as foods were more easily boiled, steamed, baked, browned, or fried. The trick, however, in using the new invention, was in learning how to regulate the heat.

Kitchen chores were made easier as more food products became available at general stores including freshly ground coffee, molasses, spices, bags of dried beans, peas, rice, and corn. Foreign trade also improved the quality and quantity of food supplies.

Additionally, new food preparation gadgets appeared, including meat grinders, apple corers, and more versatile butter churns. China, flatware, and drinking containers, however, changed very little.

Great strides were made in food preservation throughout the 19th century. In

1809 Nicholas Appert, a Frenchman, discovered that if food products, including meat and milk, were placed in a wide mouth glass bottle and then carefully corked and heated to a boiling point, the foods would not spoil. Then in 1819 the tin canister for protecting food was patented in England by Peter Durand. The food storage closet or pie safe was invented to protect fresh foods. Lined with tin or built with wire sides and tin, zinc, or wire doors for ventilation, the closet was located in a cool place and used for short-term storage of perishables such as meats, cream, or recently prepared dishes.

Natural ice, by 1820, was an article of commerce and used widely to preserve foods. It was shipped from New England to as far away as India, packed in sawdust for transportation. And even though the first icebox was patented around 1803, most Floridians could still not afford the luxury.

In 1821 when the Americans arrived in St. Augustine they were disappointed with what they found. Buildings were decaying, garbage was in the streets, and empty lots were overgrown. Those who had remained were subsisting on bare essentials. Although there were plenty of fish and citrus trees, the population had little in the way of fresh produce to feed either themselves or the new settlers. Before the Americans could remedy the situation, however, an even more critical problem sailed into the harbor.

In mid-1821 a ship from Cuba crossed the bar into Matanzas Bay and disembarked more than its passengers. Within days yellow fever raged through the town attacking newcomers, yet strangely by-passing the locals.

The cause of yellow fever was unknown, but because the locals of St. Augustine had been spared, word spread north regarding the puzzling occurrence. The conclusion drawn was that St. Augustine was a healthy place to live. As publicity filled northern newspapers, hundreds planned visits south, especially during the winter months. This phenomenal interest in old St. Augustine gave rise to what would one day become the number one industry in Florida—tourism. It is interesting to note that the word "tourist" was not used to describe 19th century visitors to St. Augustine. St. Augustinians called them "strangers," a term that followed them throughout the 1800s. As cold weather froze the north, "strangers" in ill health seeking warmer temperatures headed to St. Augustine, hoping to regain good health.

One such stranger was Ralph Waldo Emerson, an aspiring literary figure. His reflections of the city were anything but complimentary. He complained of the laziness of the people and the lack of food, yet his writings give a view of the daily routine of the town.

> I met some Indians in the street selling venison. I asked the man where he lived.
> "Yonder."
> "Where?"
> "In the big swamp."
> He sold his haunch for 5 bits.
> *Ralph Waldo Emerson, 1827*

Wild Game and "Stranger" Fare

Seminole Haunch Burgers

2 lb venison, ground (or beef)
3 T pepper
1 lg tomato, thinly sliced
1 lg onion, thinly sliced
1/2 c datil pepper sauce
loaf of hard bread, sliced, toasted

Combine venison and pepper and mix well. Shape into 8 patties about 3/4" thick. Place patties on grill 4" from coals. Grill 5 minutes on each side. Baste once with datil pepper sauce. Serve venison on bread topped with a slice of onion and tomato. Yields 4-8 servings.

Settlers' Squirrel Stew

1 squirrel, cut up
2 bay leaves, crushed
1 c onions, thinly sliced
1/4 c cornmeal
1/2 c whiskey
1 T pepper
1 t salt
1/4 c oil
2 c water

In large kettle dredge squirrel in meal, salt, and pepper then brown in oil. Add onions and brown. Add remaining ingredients, cover, and simmer 1 hour. Yields 2 servings.

American Creamed Rabbit

2 rabbits, cut in chunks
1/4 c flour
lemon juice
2 c cream
salt and pepper to taste
1/4 c oil
1 onion, thinly sliced

Sprinkle meat with lemon juice then dredge in flour, salt, and pepper. Simmer in oil about 40 minutes, stirring occasionally. Place in a greased casserole dish and add cream. Top with onions. Bake at 425° for 20 minutes. Yields 4-6 servings.

Six Mile Swamp Bull Frog Legs

If you've never been frog gigging, you've missed a treat. Get a pair of high-top rubber boots, a lantern, and a gig or spear. Wait until late at night then head into the swamp with an experienced gigger. After you've captured ten frogs, cut off back legs, wash, and skin. Discard the remainder of the frog. Pour a little lemon juice over legs and let sit overnight.

20 frogs legs
1/2 c lemon juice
1 T salt
4 t dry mustard
4 eggs
2 c cornmeal
1 t basil
1 T pepper
1/2 c oil

Remove frog legs from lemon juice and pat dry. In small bowl beat eggs. Add mustard and mix well. In another bowl combine cornmeal and seasonings. Dip legs into egg then cornmeal. Fry in oil until golden brown and crisp. Drain. Yields 2 servings.

The Andrew Anderson family from New York settled in St. Augustine in the 1820s. They lamented to relatives in a letter north that although they had plenty of good food, their table often lacked "fine white bread." That was an understandable problem because the American pioneers had yet to find time to farm the outlying region. Until they established farms, many of their provisions had to be imported including oats, wheat flour, corn, beef, and its by-product, butter. The lack of Florida beef would change, however, with the advent of the Florida cowboy.

Food for the Florida Cowboy and the Florida Cracker

The cattle industry was born in North America when the Spanish introduced their domesticated Andalusian into La Florida. Those scrawny creatures took to the landscape and thrived in the scrub country. In the 1700s when the Seminole Indians migrated to La Florida they adapted easily to cattle raising which in turn increased the herds. After La Florida became a United States territory, settlers accepted the government's offer of free land and crossed the St. Mary's River into Florida in great numbers. Conflicts arose, however, when the United States did not acknowledge the land and the cattle the Indians claimed as theirs. That, in turn, disrupted trading between the Indians and the pioneers.

Raising cattle spread across the peninsula as Florida's newest pioneers tried their hand at cattle ranching. The south's first cowboys were rough, tough, men who rode hard and ate heartily. They preferred the name "cow hunter" to the western term "cowboy." Tradition has it that the term "Florida Cracker" originated during this period because cow hunters "cracked" their whips when herding their cattle. That's a colorful account; however, the term "cracker" predates Florida and can be traced back to Shakespeare's writings. In any case, today's "Florida Cracker" is thoroughly native, somewhat country, and earnestly connected to the land.

Cow hunters exhilarated in outdoor living, leaving their women at home to do the chores. Envied by many, the Florida cow hunter's life was filled with strong drink and poker, wild beasts and black nights.

Bootstrap Jerky

5 lbs meat, beef, venison, or pork
3 t salt
1 t pepper
1 lg onion, grated
3 cloves garlic, crushed
3 T datil pepper sauce
1 c water

Slice meat with grain into 1/8" strips. Remove fat and boil until cooked through. Marinate overnight in the above ingredients. The next day remove meat and place on a rack on top of a long pan. Grill or bake in oven with door slightly open at 200° for 2-3 hours or until strips are black. Yields 40 servings.

Grilled Andalusian Steak

2 lbs flank steak
1 T dry mustard
1 T pepper
1 t salt
1/2 c chili sauce
1/3 c oil
1/2 c whiskey
4 cloves garlic, minced
1 med onion, chopped

Combine all ingredients in a pot and marinate overnight. The next day remove steaks from marinade, discard liquid, and grill steaks over hot coals 5-10 minutes on each side. Yields 2-4 servings.

Besides eating bear, raccoon, opossum, and beaver, wild hog was a favorite among Florida Crackers. Catching wild hogs was a dangerous and rousing sport, but the risk was worth it. Wild hog added a variety of rich foods to the table including lard, sausage, feet, chit'lins, head, and even brains!

North River Wild Hog Rump

Stew:
1 hog rump, cubed
2 c water
1 c rice
2 c tomatoes, crushed
2 lg onions, sliced
1 T datil pepper sauce
1 t salt
1/2 t pepper
3 T lard

Marinade:
1 T parsley
1/2 t thyme
1 carrot, thickly sliced
salt and pepper to taste
2 cloves garlic, minced
2 c red wine vinegar
1 onion, thinly sliced
2 bay leaves
1/4 c lard

Marinade: Combine ingredients in large pot and marinate hog rump overnight.

Stew: Next day remove meat and discard marinade. Wipe meat dry and set aside. In iron kettle brown onions, garlic, and meat in lard. Add remaining ingredients and simmer 1 hour or until meat is tender. Stir occasionally. Yields 4-6 servings.

Backwoods Kettle Pork Sausage

1 lb sausage, sliced
1 bell pepper, cored, diced
1 red bell pepper, cored, diced
1 onion, diced
1 c rice
1 T pepper
1 t salt
2 T datil pepper sauce

1 lg turnip, diced
3 c tomatoes, crushed
3 c water

In large iron kettle cook sausage until almost done then add vegetables and stir until brown. Pour off grease and add remaining ingredients. Bring to a boil, stir well, then simmer 45 minutes. Yields 4-6 servings.

Wild and Spicy Hog Feet

8 hog feet, dehooved
8 c water
3 datil peppers, whole
2 t sugar
8 bay leaves
1 T basil
1 T oregano
1 lg onion, quartered
8 c red wine vinegar
1 T cloves
2 T pepper
2 T salt

Place meat and water in a large kettle and boil for approximately 20-30 minutes. Reserve 4 c of liquid. Discard the remainder. In pot combine all ingredients and simmer for 30 minutes. After feet have cooked, let cool, then pour into storage vessels. Yields 8 servings.

Cracker Chit'lins

Chit'lins is "slang" for chitterlings, the small intestines of hogs or pigs which have been prepared for eating. To prepare this Cracker favorite, gut the hog then boil its small intestines in salted water until tender, approximately 30 minutes. Drain, dry, and grind up.

1 lb chit'lins, prepared as above
1 T salt
1 T pepper
1 c cornmeal, sifted
1/4 c lard

In large bowl combine all ingredients. Heat lard in skillet and fry chit'lins until crunchy, stirring occasionally. Yields 4-6 servings.

Hog Head Pudding

Pudding:
1 hog head
1 hog liver
1 T pepper
1 t salt
2 c broth from boiling water

Crust:
1 c flour
1/2 c water
1 T baking powder
1 T baking soda
1 t salt

Pudding: In large pan place head and liver and cover with water. Boil until tender, approximately 1 hour. Reserve liquid. Remove meat from head and grind up with liver. Place meat and remaining ingredients in a large bowl and mix well. Pour into a greased baking dish.

Crust: Combine all ingredients and spread evenly over meat. Bake at 350° until brown. Yields 4-6 servings.

Cracklin' Corn Pone

Cracklin' is slang for "crackling," the crisp bits that remain after rendering fat from frying or roasting the skin of a hog or pig.

1 c cracklin', prepared in advance
1/4 c lard
1 T lard
1-1/2 c buttermilk
1 egg
2 c cornmeal, self-rising

Combine milk, egg, and cornmeal until well mixed. Add 1 T lard and cracklin' then stir well. Heat the remaining lard in iron skillet then add mixture to skillet. Bake in skillet at 375° 25-30 minutes. Yields 6-8 servings.

Open Range Fried Corn

4 c corn
1 c cream
1 T pepper
1/2 lb salt pork

Fry salt pork until brown. Add corn and stir. Reduce heat and simmer 15 minutes, covered. Remove from heat and add pepper and cream. Blend well. Yields 2-4 servings.

Ximenez-Fatio House

Boarding House and Hotel Fare

In the 1820s steamships replaced sailing vessels, plying the inland waterways of Florida, particularly the wide St. Johns River. Because this mode of transportation was more efficient and convenient than sailing, traveling to St. Augustine became easier especially for the ill. Many believed that St. Augustine provided their last hope for a healthy life because it offered pure air, fresh ocean breezes, and healing sunshine. Usually invalids spent the winter months in St. Augustine, arriving in December and staying until April.

The expanding stream of sickly "strangers" created a need for available living quarters. At first families rented rooms, then boarding houses opened, one of the first around 1830 by Mrs. Samuel Cook of Charleston, South Carolina. As many as 24 guests were able to stay at her inn, today known as the Ximenez-Fatio House.

Margaret's Delicious Pot Roast

1 chuck roast
2 cloves garlic
1 c whiskey
1 c onion, quartered
4 green bell peppers, cored, quartered
4 carrots, thickly sliced
4 potatoes, quartered
1 T pepper
1 t salt
2 c black coffee, strong
2 c water
1/2 c oil

Slit roast through and stuff with onion and garlic. Place meat in large kettle and pour whiskey over roast making sure it drains into the slits. Marinate 2 days. Drain liquid from pot, add oil, and brown. Add remaining ingredients and simmer, covered, for 2 hours. Yields 6 servings.

Boarding House Fried Chicken

2 lg chickens, cut into pieces
2 t datil pepper sauce
2 t salt
1 T pepper
1 t dry mustard
1 t chili peppers
1 t thyme
1 t dill
1 t basil
1 t rosemary
1 c flour
1/2 c milk
2 eggs
1 c oil
2 c buttermilk

Marinate chicken overnight in buttermilk and datil pepper sauce. Next day discard liquid and pat chicken dry. Combine all seasonings with flour in bag sturdy enough to shake chicken. Beat eggs and milk. Shake each piece of chicken in flour, dip in egg mixture, then again in flour. Heat oil in an iron skillet over medium heat. Fry chicken, covered, turning once, until dark golden brown, about 15 minutes for dark meat, 10 minutes for white. Yields 6 servings.

St. Augustine Squash Pie

1 lb squash, sliced
2 c water
1/4 c butter, melted
1/2 c sugar
1 egg, beaten
1 T cornstarch
salt and pepper to taste
1 pastry shell, unbaked

Boil squash until tender. Drain. Mix remaining ingredients. Blend with squash then pour into crust. Bake at 350° 25-30 minutes or until mixture thickens. Yields 6 servings.

The sabal or cabbage palm is Florida's state tree. The heart of the palm tree, once a staple among early residents, beginning with Native Americans, is now illegal to harvest. For when the heart is cut from any palm, it means death for the tree. Today heart palms are commercially cultivated in Central and South America and are available in many supermarkets.

Palm Heart Salad or "Swamp Cabbage"

3 c palm hearts, sliced
1 T mustard seed
1/2 c sugar
1 sm green bell pepper, cored, shredded
1 sm onion, shredded
1 t salt
1 t celery seed
1/2 c water
1/4 c vinegar

Place palm hearts in a flat serving bowl. Spread onion and bell pepper on top. Do not stir. In saucepan bring all other ingredients to a boil. Cool then pour over vegetables. Yields 4-6 servings.

The foods in St. Augustine were conducive to good health as was the climate, as George Archibald McCall remarked when writing home.

> Do you not envy us a climate so genial, so productive? Wild fruits are everywhere: cultivated fruits are wherever you will plant them and attend to them. Melons are already ripe . . . and you may have several crops in the course of the year.
>
> George Archibald McCall, 1830

Watermelon Patch Pickles

1 med watermelon
2 t lime juice
1/2 c ginger root
5 lbs sugar
4 c white vinegar (or more)
1/4 c allspice
1/4 c cloves
water

Cut rind then cover with water. Add lime and soak overnight. Next morning wash and drain. Cover again with cold water and let stand 1 hour. Drain. Cover in a large pot once again with fresh water adding ginger and vinegar. Boil on low for 1 hour, covered, until tender. Remove ginger. Heat sugar in water until dissolved. Add spices to syrup and boil 10 minutes. Add rind and cook until clear, about 30 minutes or longer. Place in sterilized jars and seal. Yields approximately 10 pints.

American pioneers discovered they had inherited a valuable resource from the Spanish—groves of orange, grapefruit, lemon, and lime. The most prominent grove owner in St. Augustine during that time was Andrew Anderson. His vast orange groves once covered the site of present-day Flagler College, extending west to the San Sebastian River. By 1830 he and other citrus growers in St. Augustine were annually exporting over 2,500,000 oranges to northern markets. Imagine the aroma of two million orange blossoms permeating the St. Augustine air.

Just as the citrus industry thrived in St. Augustine, so did tourism. As more and more visitors journeyed south, word spread of Florida's crystal springs, its expansive forests, and its exceptionally beautiful wilderness.

Hearing of the fabled natural wonders of the region, the renowned wildlife artist, John James Audubon, set out on foot to explore the peninsula. While spending time in St. Augustine in 1834, he described a pleasant walk he took through the Anderson groves to the old wooden bridge that crossed Maria Sanchez Creek near present-day King Street.

> My dog began to run briskly around, having met with ground on which he had hunted before, and taking a direct course, led us to the great causeway that crosses the marshes at the back of the town. We refreshed ourselves with the produce of the first orange tree that we met with and in half an hour more arrived at our hotel.
>
> John James Audubon, 1834

City Hotel Orange Treat

12 slices bread, toasted
1/4 c orange juice
1/2 c pine nuts, finely chopped
1/3 c butter, softened
2 T orange rind, finely grated
1/3 c brown sugar, packed

Spread bread with butter. Combine remaining ingredients, mixing well. Spread 1 T mixture over each slice of bread. Bake at 350° for 2-3 minutes or until sugar mixture melts. Yields 6-12 servings.

According to John James Audubon's journal, he stayed at a hotel in St. Augustine. There were only two commercial houses at the time: the Union Hotel, located on the bayfront and the City Hotel.

Union Hotel Batter Cakes

1 c cornmeal
2 T butter
1/2 c water, boiling
3/4 t baking soda
1 c flour
2 t baking powder
1 egg, beaten
1/4 c milk, soured
1/4 c oil

In a large bowl combine water, cornmeal, butter, soda, and milk. Sift in flour and baking powder. Beat well. Stir in egg and beat thoroughly. Heat oil in skillet and drop in mixture by spoonfuls. Cook until brown. Yields 4-6 servings.

To mitigate increased tension between the Americans and the Seminoles, United States officials met with Seminole lead-ers near the former site of John Moultrie's Bella Vista Plantation to present the 1823 Treaty of Moultrie Creek. Seventy Seminole chiefs and warriors attended that historic event while 32 chiefs signed the compromise. In exchange for the Seminoles' relocation to south Florida, the United States promised to provide the Indians with transportation, livestock, food, cash, and a school. Most of the Seminoles accepted the government's offer; others refused and returned to the Ocala region of Florida.

For a few years, peace settled across Florida until the Americans grasped deeper into the southern territory where the Seminoles had moved in 1823. The Indians became furious. More disheartening, though, was the fact that the government refused to uphold the terms of the treaty. Unable to resolve their disagreement over ownership of the land, the Second Seminole Indian War began in 1835.

The years moved forward with Indian skirmishes and full scale military battles. Even thought intermittent winter freezes and bugs destroyed the citrus groves and Indians burned crops and settlements, determined pioneers replanted and rebuilt. They had moved to Florida—permanently—and nothing was going to make them leave.

As well, the influx of invalids and their companions continued. In 1835 St. Augustine's Examiner *notified its readers that there were now 300 accommodations available for tourists with the addition of the Florida House Hotel. This four-story wooden structure was located on the northeast corner of St. George and Treasury Streets and remained a popular ac-*

Florida House Hotel

commodation for guests until it was destroyed by fire in 1914.

Hotel dining was similar to the boarding house style of serving food. Tables seated large numbers of guests. Food was prepared in outdoor kitchens and placed "home style" in the middle of the dining table. Mounds of chicken and rice, plates of steaming vegetables, and typical southern cuisine such as rhubarb, green tomatoes, and, invariably, grits, were passed from guest to guest.

Florida House Black-Eyed Peas and Rice

2 c black-eyed peas
5 c chicken broth
1 c rice
2 carrots, thinly chopped
2 T red wine vinegar
1 t salt
1 T pepper

Combine liquids and spices, then divide equally into 2 saucepans. Bring both to boil over high heat. Add peas to one pan and simmer 45 minutes. Add rice to the other pan, cover and simmer 30-40 minutes. Add carrots to peas and cook until tender, about 10-12 minutes. Drain. Combine all ingredients. Yields 6-8 servings.

Boarding House Reach Vegetable Casserole

4 c corn
1 c green beans, thinly sliced
1/2 c green bell pepper, cored, chopped
1/4 c celery, thinly sliced
1 lg onion, thinly sliced
1/4 c water
1/2 t pepper
1/2 c sharp cheese, finely grated
1 c cream

Combine all ingredients and pour into a greased casserole dish. Bake at 350° for 35-45 minutes. Yields 6-8 servings.

Southern Green Tomato Pie

6 tomatoes, green, thinly sliced
2 T butter
1/4 c white sugar
2 onions, thinly sliced
salt and pepper to taste
2 pastry shells

Place half of the tomatoes into one shell and sprinkle lightly with salt. Add half of the onions and sprinkle with half of the sugar. Dot with 1 T butter. Repeat layering. Sprinkle top layer with pepper. Cover pie with other shell, pricking with a fork. Bake at 350° for about 45 minutes, or until crust is brown. Yields 4-6 servings.

Tasty Rhubarb Nut Bread

Bread:
1-1/2 c rhubarb, diced
1-1/2 c brown sugar, packed
2/3 c oil
1 t vanilla
1 egg
2-1/2 c flour, sifted
1 c milk, soured
1 t soda
1 t salt
1/2 c pine nuts, finely chopped

Topping:
1/2 c sugar
1 T butter

Bread: Stir ingredients together one at a time. Pour into 2 well greased and floured loaf pans, filling each 2/3 full.

Topping: Blend ingredients then spread evenly over each bread. Bake at 325° for 45-55 minutes. Yields 2 loaves.

Grits St. Augustine Style

2 c grits, cooked
1/2 c sharp cheese, grated
1 onion, diced
1 c tomatoes, crushed
1 lb sausage, ground, cooked
1/4 c oil

Cook onions in oil until translucent. Layer a well-greased baking dish in this order using half the ingredients: sausage, grits, onions, tomatoes, cheese. Repeat and bake at 325° until brown. Yields 4 servings.

After dinner at the Florida House Hotel, the women relaxed in the parlor where they sipped tea, tasted delicate sweets, and chatted of children, fashions, and their health. The men would remain in the dining room or retire to the verandah to snack on peanuts, smoke Cuban hand-rolled cigars, and discuss timely events.

Verandah Peanuts

4 qts peanuts, raw, unshelled
6 qts water
6 T salt

Combine all ingredients, bring to a boil and slow boil 3-4 hours. Peanuts are ready to eat when they are soft and juicy. Drain. Yields 4 quarts.

Florida's Sorrel Pie

Either sheep sorrel or wood sorrel (oxalis) leaves or wild oxalis seed pods may be used.

1 handful sorrel leaves or 1/2 c seed pods
1/2 c butter, softened
5 eggs, well beaten
2 c brown sugar
1 T flour
2 pastry shells, unbaked

Cream butter and sugar. Add remaining ingredients. Mix well and pour into shell. Cover with second shell, making slits in top. Bake at 325° about 30 minutes or until golden brown and set. Yields 6 servings.

Wildflower Tea Muffins

2 c blossoms, rose or dandelion
1/2 c butter, softened
1 c light brown sugar, packed
1 egg
1 c milk
1/2 t baking soda
2 c flour

Cream together butter and sugar. Add egg. Combine milk and soda and add to mixture. Add flour. Gingerly stir in blossoms then fill muffin tins 2/3 full. Bake 20 minutes at 350°. Yields 6-8 servings.

Dandelion Tea

4 c dandelion roots
4 c water
1 c honey

Dig roots then scrub thoroughly. Roast at 300° for several hours until brown. Grind then add to water and simmer 30 minutes. Add honey and stir well. Dilute mixture to taste. Yields 4-6 servings.

By 1840 there were at least three hotels in St. Augustine and a handful of boarding houses. Cooks from these establishments daily visited private shops or the public market to supply fresh foods for their tables. They competed for the "strangers" that came to town, priding themselves on serving the finest cuisine and offering the most comfortable accommodations.

On market day the public market at the eastern end of the Plaza would fill with hawkers trading cloth, leather goods, or household supplies. Vendors in individual wooden stalls lined the sides of the building's interior, protected during the frequent rains. The public market had been in the same location since the First Spanish Period and had always been a gathering place for visits and to compare produce and prices.

As the Second Seminole Indian War continued, the United States demanded removal of all Seminoles from Florida. The Indians answered the government's demand by stepping up their raids, burning settlements, farms, and military outposts. Osceola, a respected Seminole spokesperson, yet only half Indian, insisted that the Seminoles would never leave. However, weak from disease and weary of battle, Osceola suggested a truce. The Americans agreed and arranged another meeting with the Seminoles near Moultrie Creek, just south of St. Augustine.

The year was 1837. Osceola and his supporters traveled from the Ocala area under a white flag of truce. When they arrived at Moultrie Creek, they were captured by American troops. They were bound, ferried across the San Sebastian River, marched across the wooden bridge at Maria Sanchez Creek, through the Andersons' orange groves, and down the narrow streets to Fort Marion. And there they were imprisoned.

Several days later, Osceola's men escaped by scaling the high coquina cell wall, loosening the iron bars in the narrow window and squeezing through to freedom. Osceola, ill with malaria, did not have the strength to follow. Fearing an attempt to free him, the government moved Osceola to Fort Moultrie in South Carolina. Within weeks Osceola, one of the most popular leaders of the Seminole Indians, died of pneumonia.

In 1842, after seven years of battle, the Second Seminole Indian War drew to a close. Property and livestock had been destroyed. Countless numbers of Indians and pioneers had died. Over 1,500 United States troops were killed, their bodies eventually moved from the graves where they had fallen to St. Augustine for burial at the cemetery adjacent to the St. Francis Barracks.

The American government believed that removing the Seminole Indians to the arid plains of Oklahoma would eliminate further problems. This mass exodus from paradise of yet another group of "Floridians," over 4,000 to be exact, was reminiscent of the tragic journey made by the Cherokee Nation of North Carolina several years earlier. The Cherokees called their path westward the "Trail of Tears." The Seminole Nation of Florida experienced the same sad fate.

Not all the Seminoles cooperated with the United States Government. Approximately 300 fled into the Everglades of south Florida.

Although unjust as it was, the removal of the Seminoles from Florida allowed the government, for the first time since gaining possession of Florida, to survey its vast interior and map its unexplored regions.

And with this inland exploration, Florida stood poised on the threshold of yet another transition and yet another beginning—Statehood.

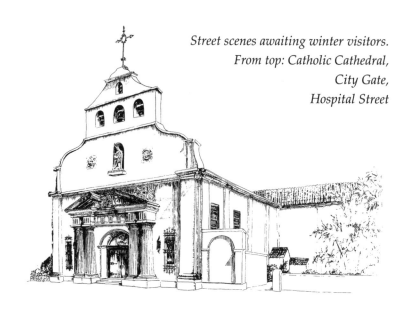

Street scenes awaiting winter visitors.
From top: Catholic Cathedral,
City Gate,
Hospital Street

Chapter VI.
The State of Florida
1845-1885

Florida entered the Union March 3, 1845 as the 27th state. Land was selling for little more than $1.25 an acre. Entrepreneurs traveled to the peninsula in hopes of making their fortune. And tourism had taken hold. Indeed, Florida was on the move.

By the late 1840s, St. Augustine was one of the most popular health resorts in America. Sickly strangers who had the financial resources to escape the frigid northern weather traveled great distances to recuperate in the Florida sun. The prominent illness during this period was tuberculosis: its standard treatment was rest, warm weather, and nutritious foods. Where else could one find those requirements but in St. Augustine, Florida?

Pale guests reclined on sofas set out in the sun. They relaxed on wide verandahs or huddled in overstuffed chairs in the parlors of the city's hotels and boarding houses. Coughing could be heard throughout the night, the death rattle of diseased lungs keeping others awake with fear. Coffin builders and grave diggers were kept busy. One writer to the city penned home that:

> . . . every public house is, to a certain extent, a hospital, and whenever you walk the streets you meet some sufferer, whose wasted form and feeble gait proclaim the victim of consumption.

But not all of the strangers who came to St. Augustine were invalids. Many came simply to visit the oldest city in the Nation. They descended the steamboat ramp on the St. John's River at Picolata, then boarded a coach for the arduous journey to St. Augustine. Two separate accounts of that trip are given.

> The ride, to a lover of nature, is charming, and not by any means monotonous. The whole distance is garlanded by flowers of every variety—lilacs, honeysuckles, azaleas, sunflowers, and a thousand varieties of small flowers which enamel the ground.

> We started in an old fashioned six horse Concord coach, seven passengers inside and three on top for our ride of 18 miles across a most desolate country, the road nearly half the time being a foot under water with an occasional piece of corduroy over hopelessly swampy places. Both coach and harness were very old and dilapidated and before we got across we had broken down four times.

It would seem that both beauty and adventure are indeed in the eyes of the beholder.

As the city's visitors increased, so did the coffers of St. Augustine and the pocketbooks of its inhabitants. Increased tourism continued to bring a need for additional accommodations. In March, 1847, the Magnolia House, located on the corner of St. George and Hypolita Streets, opened. Within six years, demand for more rooms in St. Augustine was so great that the owner of the inn had to increase his rooms from 17 to 45. The Magnolia House was three stories high, constructed of wood, with long verandahs on both levels to capture the ocean breeze. It remained a major tourist hostelry until it burned in 1926.

One visitor to the Magnolia House was displeased with his accommodations and wrote of his stay with less than a favorable description.

> It would seem that all the old women & ugly children in the United States come to St. Augustine; & the ugliest of them stop at the Magnolia.

The foods St. Augustinians ate did not change much until after the Civil War. Then diets were enhanced with the addition of pre-packaged foods such as Hershey's chocolate bars which sold for 10¢ in the early 1880s. General stores were opening, their shelves stocked with rock candy, candy sticks, and canned foods such as corn, tomatoes, syrup, guava jelly, and Pet Milk. No new spices were added during this period, but commonly used spices were more readily available. These included, for example, lemon and orange extract, dried ginger, mustard, and cinnamon.

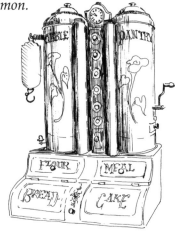

Portable Pantry

Outdoor kitchens remained in use as did the slow-cooking wood-eating monster which, by this time, had been improved. Especially useful were its water reservoirs which supplied hot water for kitchen clean-up.

Churns and grinders were also improved. A cream separator was invented that reduced the average 2-3 day process. Hand-cranked coffee grinders could be purchased for home use and tin storage boxes came in assorted sizes and shapes. These culinary-related advancements contributed to an easier domestic life for women.

Although experimentation with artificial refrigeration began as early as 1748, it was not until 1844 that a machine was constructed that would eventually revolutionize the food industry. The machine was invented in Apalachicola, Florida by Dr. John Gorrie, who needed the coolness to ease his malaria patients. When he tried to sell the idea to entrepreneurs in the north, it was rejected. The New York Times ran an article reporting that someone from the south "thought he could make ice better than God Himself."

By 1856 the use of commercial refrigeration became widespread in the north where it was used for meat-packing and brewing. Enoch Piper of Maine was granted a U.S. patent for the first practical method of artificially freezing fish.

By the early 1880s railroads were using cold storage cars for transporting meats and produce, but ice was still too costly for most Floridians to import.

Food containers improved with John Mason's 1858 invention of the glass jar for home canning. Constructed of heavier weight glass than commercial food jars, the Mason Jar could withstand processing temperatures in boiling water canners or pressure canners.

In 1860, Louis Pasteur of France proved that bacteria was associated with food spoilage. This discovery spurred improvements in the development of lids to seal storage jars. But older methods of protecting against spoilage, salting, drying, and pickling remained effective preservation techniques as well.

Deliciously Palatable Food for the Afflicted

Tolomato River Crab Soup

1 lb crab meat
1 c cream
4 c milk
1 t salt
1/2 c flour
1/4 c butter
1 t white pepper
1 c turkey or chicken broth
1/3 c sherry

Melt butter in saucepan then blend in flour until smooth. Slowly add broth, stirring constantly until smooth. Allow to cook on low for 3 minutes. Add milk and cream, stirring continually for 1 minute. Add remaining ingredients and cook on low until thoroughly heated. Yields 4-6 servings.

Picolata Deer Soup

2 lbs deer, cubed
8 c water
1 T pepper
4 c tomatoes, crushed
1 T salt
2 T oregano
2 c turnips, cubed
3 T parsley
1 c onion, diced
2 c carrots, sliced

Simmer deer in water for 1 hour. Remove from heat and allow to stand overnight until fat congeals. The following day, remove and discard fat.

In large kettle combine meat, broth, and remaining ingredients. Simmer 1 hour. Yields 6-8 servings.

The rate by the week at the Magnolia House was $6.50 for a single room on the second floor, food not included. Food was extra and could cost up to $4.00 a week for the best selection. A room in the attic for one week cost $4.50. If a "stranger" desired a fireplace, the price was negotiated. Any visitor wishing an extra meal was charged 37-1/2¢ for each. One traveler to St. Augustine complained that she had to pay a ridiculous price for a room that didn't even have a carpet in it.

Matanzas River Shrimp Soup

3 lbs shrimp, shelled
1 c potatoes, peeled, diced
3/4 c salt pork, diced
1 t salt
1 T flour
1 t pepper
1/2 c onions, diced
1 c water
1 c cream

In a large kettle fry salt pork and onions until brown. Add flour and brown. Add remaining ingredients, except shrimp and cream, cover, and simmer 30 minutes. Add shrimp and simmer 10 minutes. Add cream and stir until heated. Yields 4-6 servings.

Florida House Vegetable Soup

8 c tomatoes, crushed
4 c beef broth
1/3 c brown sugar
2 c beef, cooked, cubed
1 c corn
1 c peas

1 c green beans
1 c onions, diced
1 T salt
1 T pepper

Combine all ingredients and simmer for 1 hour. Yields 10-12 servings.

By 1855, Miss Louisa Fatio had bought the boarding house which had been owned by Mrs. Margaret Cook. She operated it as a fashionable establishment until her death in 1875. One gentleman described Miss Fatio's inn as having "homelike and comfortable" lodgings. Of Miss Fatio he remarked that she was "a most estimable and popular lady."

Louisa's Fine Potato Soup

3 potatoes, cubed
2 t salt
3 c milk
1 c cream
1 onion, diced
1 T pepper
2 T datil pepper sauce
2 T flour
3 T butter
2 c water

Combine potatoes, onion, water, and spices in a large pot. Simmer, covered, until potatoes are mushy. Remove from heat and stir rapidly, blending until smooth. Add remaining ingredients, return to heat, and stir briskly. Simmer until thoroughly heated. Yields 4-6 servings.

Wooden Roller

Cucumber Soup

2 lg cucumbers, peeled, diced
1 sm onion, diced
2 c chicken broth
1/2 c cream
2 T lime juice
1 t salt
1 t pepper
1/2 c water

In a small saucepan combine water, spices, and onion and simmer 15 minutes. Add cucumber and chicken stock, cover, and simmer 20 minutes. Remove from heat and allow to cool. Transfer to a large mixing bowl and whisk until well blended and pulverized. Add cream and lime juice and beat well. Yields 2 servings.

Fruit Soup

It is your choice as to the fruit you use—or you might want to experiment with a combination of several.

4 c fruit, sliced
3 c water
1 t salt
1 T sugar
1 T flour

Combine all ingredients, except flour, and cook on low for 20-30 minutes. Strain to remove skin and seeds. Return to heat and stir in flour to thicken. Set aside until cool. Stir briskly. Yields 4-8 servings.

Another famous writer to visit St. Augustine during this time was Washington Irving. So impressed by the natural bounty of the region, he wrote:

> . . . The spontaneous fruits of the earth furnished subsistence without toil.
> Washington Irving, 1855

Guava trees were imported to St. Augustine from south Florida. Because the guava was native to tropical climes, it had to be carefully tended during St. Augustine's winter months, which, on occasion, were bitingly cold.

Florida Guava Jelly

1 c guava, seeds removed, mashed
3 c honey
1/2 c pectin
paraffin

Combine fruit and honey in saucepan. Bring to a boil, stirring constantly. Add pectin and boil hard for 1 minute, stirring constantly. Remove from heat, skim off foam, then pour into sterilized glass jars. Cover with 1/8" hot paraffin. Yields approximately 2 pints.

Guava Pudding

2 c guava, seeds removed, mashed
3/4 c white sugar
1/4 c water
1 c butter, melted
3 c flour, sifted
1 c cream
4 eggs, well beaten
2 c brown sugar
1 T vanilla

Combine guava, water, and white sugar and blend well. Pour into a well-greased baking dish. Heat in oven until bubbly, but be careful not to burn mixture. Remove from oven.

In a separate bowl combine remaining ingredients and mix well. Pour over guava mixture, place back in the oven and bake at 350° for 30 minutes or until brown. Yields 6-8 servings.

By 1850 Florida had over 87,000 residents. St. Augustine also had gained in permanent settlers while maintaining its status as a popular resort for the curious, the rich, and the ailing. During this growth period new problems arose with the Seminoles who had moved to south Florida in 1842. From 1855 to 1858, the Indians and Americans fought. Finally, as a last resort, the federal government bribed the Indians with the promise of great sums of money and free transportation to Oklahoma. When the Seminoles accepted this offer, the third and final Seminole Indian War ended.

Hundreds of Seminoles who once referred to themselves as "A jia tki" or "the white corn people," relocated west. However, several hundred Seminoles again fled deep into the swamps of the Everglades. Today many of their descendants continue to maintain the noble traditions of their elders.

With the end of one conflict, another began—the fermenting issue was slavery. Discussion among the southern states regarding secession from the Union widened a growing chasm between north and south, between religious denominations, and within families. Such was the case in St. Augustine. As talk of northern aggression occurred over dinner and drinks, hostile feelings arose, especially when Abraham Lincoln won the 1860 election. Although only a few St. Augustinians owned slaves, a

critical economic dilemma regarding the issue of slavery shadowed the city: If the southern states rebelled against the federal government over slavery, what would happen to the northern "stranger" industry in St. Augustine?

In January, 1861 that question was put to the test with the peal of the church bells at the Catholic Church. St. Augustinians and strangers gathered side by side in the Plaza that cold morning to learn that Florida was the third state to secede from the Union.

Washerwoman

Government House

The Magnolia House raised the south's flag of secession—the fifth flag to fly over the oldest town in America. Although the flag of dissension and separation boldly announced where the Magnolia House proprietor stood on the issue of secession, many "strangers" remained throughout that winter, so desperate were they to recover from their illness.

While the Confederate flag flew over St. Augustine, loyalties split families and friends. Youthful men marched exuberantly forth to join the side which best represented their position on slavery.

In March, 1862, when the first federal ship anchored just east of St. Augustine, the town leaders prepared to surrender. Fort Marion hoisted the white flag of truce as federal troops rowed their gunboat toward the city basin. Disembarking, the men in blue were cordially greeted by the town mayor and escorted to Government House. After city officials heard the terms of surrender, the federal officers were invited to dine at the Florida House Hotel where they were served, among other things, coffee brewed from sweet pota-

toes. Throughout the war federal troops occupied St. Augustine. Northern sympathizers, southern sympathizers, and Yankee soldiers co-existed in a strained but tranquil peace.

During this period, Northern visitors no longer ventured south. This created the economic crisis St. Augustine had feared. Ironically, though, the loss of income from the sickly strangers was somewhat mitigated by income earned from satisfying the robust appetites of the Yankees in uniform. Hotels, boarding houses, and families often fed the soldiers. In turn, the army sold supplies to the St. Augustinians who swore allegiance to the United States. However, the army did not allow local merchants to sell provisions to those who refused to take the oath.

January 1, 1863 marked a rare day in St. Augustine's history. It was the date that President Abraham Lincoln's Emancipation Proclamation was read to a group of former slaves who had congregated at an empty lot on St. George Street. The message of freedom was received with mixed emotions. While many African Americans continued to live and work with their former owners, others moved to a wooded area west of Maria Sanchez Creek along present-day Washington Street. These Freedmen built humble dwellings, planted small gardens, and named their free community Africa. This free community of African Americans was the first in St. Augustine since 1739 when governing officials of the First Spanish Period encouraged Africans to build their free town at Fort Mose.

Fighting became so horrendous toward the end of the Civil War that the Union army established additional hospitals throughout the south. One in St. Augustine was established in the home of Lucy Abbott, on the Fort Green. The women of St. Augustine, disregarding their southern sympathies, moved swiftly to volunteer their services to the injured. They prepared nutritious foods at their homes and boarding houses and personally delivered them to the hospital.

Louisa Fatio's Curlew Soup

The Whimbrel Curlew is a large gray-brown wading bird with a long decurved bill. It lives along the shores, mud flats, and marshes of Florida. Considered a migratory fowl, it can no longer be hunted.

1 curlew, prepared (or chicken for today's
   cook)
6 c water
1 T salt
1 T pepper
1 onion, diced
2 T datil pepper sauce
1 c rice
1 carrot, thinly sliced

Combine all ingredients in a large kettle, except rice, cover, and simmer 2 hours. Debone meat and return to kettle. Add rice and simmer 30-40 minutes or until rice is tender. Yields 4-6 servings.

Soup Tureen

Throughout the Civil War years, Clarissa and Andrew Anderson's son, Andrew, attended medical school in the north. The Andersons attempted to remain neutral during the war.

Clarissa Anderson's Arrowroot Porridge

Arrowroot is a wild plant which Clarissa collected from the marsh at the back of her property. The root was considered to have medicinal value.

1 c arrowroot root, finely chopped
1 c potatoes, diced
3 c water
1 T pepper
1 t salt
1 c cream

Boil root in water and salt until half the liquid has evaporated. Add pepper and potatoes, cover, and simmer for 45 minutes. Stir in cream and heat thoroughly. Yields 2 servings.

Mrs. Frances Smith was the mother of Confederate General Edmund Smith. Her loyalties obviously were with the southern campaign, yet her compassion permitted her to help those in need.

Mrs. Smith's
Boiled Custard

4 c milk
3/4 c sugar
1 T flour, heaping
4 eggs
1 t vanilla

In a saucepan on low, stir flour and sugar. Add eggs and stir well. Add milk, increase heat, and stir constantly until mixture boils. Immediately reduce heat, continuing to stir. When mixture coats the spoon, remove from heat. Add vanilla. As it cools, it will thicken. Yields 4 servings.

Florida was important during the Civil War because its mild climate and rich soil contributed to a healthy food supply for the Confederate troops. Salt for preservation of meats was collected in giant iron cauldrons by boiling sea water until it evaporated leaving behind white crystals. These massive pots are often seen at historical sites along the coast of Florida.

Several months after the explosive conclusion of the Civil War, St. Augustine quietly marked its 300th anniversary. But there was little to celebrate. The city was like the rest of the South — it was in complete disarray.

One visitor to St. Augustine wrote that:

> *... the whole South is in a terribly dilapidated condition at Present.*

Chaos overtook St. Augustine as Confederate soldiers slowly returned home to discover that their personal property had been confiscated by the United States government. The depression that overshadowed the people of St. Augustine during the Civil War had caused them to neglect their town. Economic disaster loomed.

As the months of healing passed, St. Augustine was ignored by northern "strangers." The defeatist attitude of the people of the oldest city in the nation exacerbated the situation. Supplies were limited and shopkeepers did not reorder. The few who visited St. Augustine found price gouging rampant. A Jacksonville, Florida newspaper warned tourists to stay away. Another visitor wrote that St. Augustine:

> *... looks as if it had fallen asleep when vacated by the Spaniards and has hardly yet begun to wake up.*

A Time of Renewal

All across Florida entrepreneurs settled, but none in St. Augustine. The once sleepy hamlet, which became quite active during the war, slid back into slumber. Then in 1869, renewed enthusiasm from tourists surfaced with the construction of the St. Augustine Hotel.

St. Augustine Hotel

It was the first hotel built since the Magnolia in 1847. Rising four stories high, the St. Augustine Hotel was wooden with gingerbread-style architecture and ideally located adjacent to the north side of the Plaza. The hotel's size, its newness, and its advertisements in northern papers enticed strangers back to St. Augustine. The wording of one advertisement promised:

> *... The dining-hall is capable of seating over 300 guests, and the table will be furnished with all the luxuries of the northern markets.*

Atlantic Spicy Shrimp and Vegetable Medley

1 lb jumbo shrimp, peeled, deveined
1 c mushrooms, sliced
1 c zucchini, thinly sliced
1 c onions, thinly sliced
1/2 c bell pepper, cored, thinly sliced
1 clove garlic, minced
2 T olive oil
1 T pepper
2 T parsley
1/2 c sherry
2 c rice, cooked

Combine all ingredients except rice. Toss to coat and let sit 1 hour. Transfer mixture to a baking dish. Bake 15 minutes at 325°. Serve over rice. Yields 2-4 servings.

Hotel St. Augustine Chicken Bordeaux

1 fryer, quartered
1/3 c flour
1 t pepper
1 t salt
1 t datil pepper sauce
3 T olive oil
1 clove garlic, minced
1/2 c mushrooms, sliced
1 c tomatoes, cubed
1 c dry white wine
1 T flour

Rub chicken with spices then dredge in flour. In skillet heat oil and garlic and lightly brown chicken. Remove chicken and add mushrooms to skillet and brown. Remove mushrooms and add tomatoes and half of the wine. Replace chicken in skillet and brown. Cover and simmer 1 hour. Remove chicken, then stir in remaining wine. Thicken with flour. Add mushrooms, stir, then add chicken. Yields 4 servings.

New York Fried Squash Blossoms

2-3 doz squash blossoms, picked just prior
    to opening
1 T flour
1/8 t pepper
1 t salt
1 c milk
1/2 c oil
1 t paprika

In a shaker jar, combine milk, flour, and salt. Place squash blossoms in large pan and gently pour the milk-flour mixture over them. Heat the oil in a large heavy skillet until a drop of water sizzles. Carefully lift blossoms from batter and gently place in skillet. Fry the batter-coated blossoms in the hot oil until golden brown. Drain on paper then sprinkle with paprika. Serve hot. Yields 8-10 servings.

Elegantly Candied Rose and Violet Petals

2 c petals, rose or violet
glycerin
4 egg whites
1 c sugar
1/4 c water

Bring water, egg whites, and sugar to a boil. Drop a handful of petals into the syrup. Boil for 1 minute without stirring. Remove pan from heat. Remove individual flowers from syrup and place on oiled dish. Spread petals apart. Drop a second handful of blossoms into the syrup and again cook for 1 minute. Continue until all flowers have been coated. Allow the crystal blossoms to set in a warm, dry place for 24 hours or until hard and dry. Store in an airtight container. Yields 12 servings.

Julia Newberry wrote in her diary of her stay at the St. Augustine Hotel.

> *We found a fine new hotel, large, clean, comfortable, and with gas in it . . . . The house has been full all the time, some nice people and a great many horrid ones.*

But not everyone agreed with the offerings of the hotel. Alice Morton Brown remarked after eating a meal at the hotel that obviously:

> *The cattle were not penned up and fattened before killing, and the beef is very tough and stringy and almost uneatable.*

By the late 1870s, Abbie Brooks, a talented writer and visitor to St. Augustine, wrote a detailed and picturesque account of her impression of the typical Florida Cracker.

> *. . . so thin a mosquito would be doing a bad business trying to obtain sustenance from their bloodless bodies . . . . Like birds of the air, they only want a roosting place when night overtakes them.*
>
> *Their houses are mostly made of logs, notched to fit at the corners, the floor oftentimes being made of earth, but usually boards are sawed by hand.*

Miss Brooks continued by stating:

> These tenements are scoured once a week, when the beds are sunned, and everything turned out.
>
> The men are not always dressed in "store clothes," with a corresponding outfit, but usually country-made cotton home-spun.
>
> The genuine Cracker wears a broad-brimmed hat, braided from palmetto, a brown jean coat and breeches, a deer-skin vest with the fur left on, and a pair of stout, useful cowskin boots or shoes.

Writer Sidney Lanier was also intrigued with the life of the Florida Cracker. While traveling by steamboat, the captain showed him a handwritten note from a Cracker who raised an old Spanish delicacy for trade. He brought his home-grown vanilla to the boat landing with the note:.

> Deer Sir
> i send you one bag Verneller, pleeze fetch one pat of shus num 8 and ef enny over fetch twelve yards hoamspin.
>
> Yrs truly

Abbie Brooks also observed that with the sociable Cracker:

> Chickens are always killed for company . . . . Your plate is piled with sweet potatoes and corn-dodger bread, or ashcake, to be washed down with strong coffee . . . .

Southern Sweet Potato Pie

1 c sweet potatoes, peeled, grated
1/4 c oil
1/2 c brown sugar
3 eggs, beaten
1 c milk
1 t vanilla
1/2 c raisins
1/2 c hickory nuts

Combine all ingredients. Grease shallow baking dish. Place mixture into dish and bake at 375° for 60 minutes. Yields 6-8 servings.

Hush Puppies or Corn Dodgers

The term "hush puppy" supposedly derived its name from the Florida Cracker cook who would try to keep her hound from whining for a bite of vitals. She'd scold, "Hush puppy, hush" every time the ole' fella would howl for a treat.

1 c cornmeal
1 t salt
1/2 c flour
1/2 c cream
1/2 c water
1 t baking powder
3 T sugar
1/2 c onion, minced
1 T datil pepper sauce
1 c oil

Combine all ingredients except oil. Drop by teaspoons into hot oil. Brown and drain. Yields 4-6 servings.

Boiled Coffee

4 c water
1/4 c coffee, coarsely ground

Combine water and coffee and boil for 20 minutes. Scrape sides of pot and reduce heat. Simmer for 5 minutes then serve. Yields 6 cups.

Throughout the 1800s, sportsmen found Florida an ideal location for hunting wild game. Winter from Home *publicized the experiences of a typical northern hunter. One item informed its readers that he always:*

> . . . takes his coffee-pot with him in preference to the brandy bottle, as the climate is unfavorable to the free use of spirits. Coffee is universally drank, and it is a sufficient stimulant in this delightful country.
> Winter from Home, 1852

As St. Augustine slowly recovered from the War Between the States, city officials began to raze the older buildings in town. This action alarmed many, including the New Jersey Sentinel. The paper reported that:

> The hand of the vandal has been pulling down the coquina houses which are or were the attraction of the place . . . . I wondered that the state, county, and city did not step in and stop the destructive tendency of Americans. St. Augustine should be a perpetual link between the past and present. While it is too late to restore what has been lost, I should think that self-interest alone would lead to an instant cessation of any further interference with what remains.
> The New Jersey Sentinel, 1875

The writer of this article would be even more disappointed to learn that since 1900, St. Augustinians have razed an additional 300 historic structures in the name of progress.

But others, such as the Andersons, not only valued the charm of antiquated buildings, they contributed to the preservation of St. Augustine's history. Indeed, the primary reason that interest was revived in St. Augustine after the war was due to the St. Augustine Hotel. Partners in the hotel included E. E. Vail, Frank Palmer, and Dr. Andrew Anderson, son of Andrew and Clarissa Anderson, who had returned from the north after the Civil War to practice medicine in St. Augustine.

The hotel had a short life, burning to the ground in 1887. Even so, the St. Augustine Hotel began a remarkable trend by attracting tourists back to town. The new breed of visitors, however, were very different: many were healthy, had inquiring minds, and were often wealthy and sometimes famous.

San Marco Hotel

Among the more prominent who casually dropped in for a short stay at the St. Augustine Hotel in 1878 were Henry Morrison Flagler, the Standard Oil millionaire from New York, and his wife, Mary Harkness. Mary needed respite from the bitter New York winter and the Flaglers had heard that Florida would be the best place to go for her recovery. The Flaglers stayed briefly in St. Augustine before returning north.

By the early 1880s St. Augustine's population was nearing 3,000. The town had two newspapers, several schools, and a skating rink. It even had a popular eatery, the Ancient City Restaurant, which proclaimed that it could prepare a meal at any hour with oysters served on short notice.

In 1884, the San Marco Hotel was built north of the City Gate. It was a dramatic wooden structure with seven-story towers from which guests could view the surrounding marshes, the Matanzas River, and Anastasia Island. A unique feature of the San Marco was its theatre where for only $1.00 a visitor could purchase for

two a dance, coffee, lemonade, and a dessert. One young woman wrote of her stay in St. Augustine that:

> I like St. Augustine, & every one does, & generally without knowing why; one is bored to death half the time, & yet fascinated with the place; it is so quaint, old, & different from any other place in America.

Many felt that same way about St. Augustine. There was something fascinating about the place, for indeed visitors returned again and again. In 1885 Henry Flagler returned, this time with his second wife, Ida Alice. His beloved Mary, mother of his three children, had died several years earlier. Henry Flagler, in his fifties, was in search of a new beginning. As he sat on the verandah of the San Marco, surrounded by gulls sweeping across the horizon, and the aroma of food drifting from the hotel's kitchen, one can only imagine what Henry Morrison Flagler was dreaming—or what he was planning.

Chapter VII.
The Gilded Age of Henry Flagler
1886-1913

*I*n 1843, Clarissa Anderson, a twenty year resident of St. Augustine, wrote to her family in the north that what the city needed was:

> *. . . an enterprising Yankee that would keep a first rate house.*
> *A good house would make money without any doubt.*

It was four decades before Clarissa's prediction would come true, but when it did, the landscape of St. Augustine changed forever. The enterprising Yankee who built that "first rate house" and then turned the eastern seaboard of Florida into the tourist mecca of the south was none other than Henry Morrison Flagler.

Hotel Ponce de Leon

On January 11, 1888, the Daily News-Herald of Jacksonville reported on Henry Flagler's first Florida pioneering achievement:

THE PONCE DE LEON OPENS.

TOURISTS GAZE IN WONDER

AT THE

HANDSOME STRUCTURE.

At precisely twelve minutes past five this afternoon a special train carrying the passengers of the vestibule train from Jacksonville, arrived in the St. Augustine station, having made the run in fifty-seven minutes. The passengers were brought in two parlor cars . . . and numbered thirty in all. An almost deafening shout of "Hotel Ponce de Leon," "San Marco" and "Magnolia Hotel" arose from the throats of two or three dozen bus and carriage drivers, and in less than five minutes the party was rolling rapidly down Cordova Street amid clouds of dust, all eager to get a glimpse of the most wonderful inn yet built in the whole world.

It was dark, and the Hotel Ponce de Leon was brilliantly lighted by electricity for the occasion. As the carriages turned sharply from Cordova Street into the private hotel driveway, the structure came into the full view of the tourists, and expressions of wonder and admiration burst involuntarily from their lips . . . .

Rotunda, Hotel Ponce de Leon

The St. Augustine society newspaper, The Tatler, described the dining room of the Ponce as:

. . . the grandest, the most magnificent, indeed persons who have traveled the world over pronounce it the most magnificent of any hotel on earth, its area is ninety by one hundred and fifty feet, and eight hundred persons may dine in it at the same time.

After the completion of Henry Flagler's magnificent Hotel Ponce de Leon, delicacies such as migratory fowl, North Atlantic seafood, caviar, and European wines flowed into St. Augustine. Most local residents had never experienced such a combination of exquisite flavors until they dined with Mr. Flagler and his guests.

Since the chefs at the Hotel Ponce de Leon demanded massive quantities of fresh foods, including vegetables, fruits, meats, and seafood, agricultural productivity increased and the seafood industry in St. Augustine was established. Bakeries opened to supply innkeepers and families with freshly baked goods. One of the first

was the Moeller Brothers City Bakery, founded in the 1880s. It operated from its wagon and then its store at 50 San Marco Avenue until 1960. The bright yellow and green horse-drawn wagon allowed an unobstructed view of the four-tiered turntables filled with pies, cake, and breads.

tation reached new heights in St. Augustine with Henry Flagler's hotels: sterling silver, gold-plated serving dishes, crystal, exquisite porcelains, and delicate linens awaited his guests. Other hotels competed with the Flagler properties as a renaissance in ancient St. Augustine began.

Wood burning stoves were modernized for use with coal. General stores offered a wider selection of spices, flour, oats, and ground meal which they stored in large metal vats or fancy tins. Fresh vegetables from local farms filled huge wooden barrels. Large crocks held salty brine in which pickles floated. Fresh meats hung from rafters in the butcher's section while sawdust covered the floor to absorb blood from meat processing.

By the early 1900s affluent families and hostelries in St. Augustine scrambled to acquire tin-lined "ice boxes" to store the precious commodity—ice. Finally available through transportation by rail or steamboat, ice blocks were delivered to homes by horse-drawn wagons as children ran behind begging for a shaving or a chip of that odd, new "food."

The Age of Technology saw the discovery of electricity which revolutionized food preparation, making cooking and kitchen chores less labor-intensive. Food presen-

Henry Flagler missed no detail in building his empire. He commissioned the famed Louis Tiffany of New York to design the stained glass windows in the palatial dining room of the Ponce. He had the last verse of a poem by William Shenstone inlaid in the floor near the broad stairs leading to the dining room. William Shenstone had etched the verse two centuries earlier on a window-pane at the Red Lion Inn at Henley-on-the-Thames, England.

Whoe'er has traveled life's dull round,
Where'er his stages may have been,
May sigh to think he still has found
His warmest welcome at an inn.

The Hotel Ponce de Leon cost $2.5 million to build, half of what the United States had paid for Florida 66 years earlier. Obviously, there was no limit to Henry Flagler's extravagance as noted not only by the design of the Ponce, but also by the opening night banquet prepared for his guests.

MENU

Blue Points

Cream Soup, à la Reine
Consommé Printanière

Hors d'œuvres, Variés
Croquettes of Shrimp, Robert

Broiled Shad, Maître d'Hôtel
Parisienne Potatoes

Roast Ribs of Beef
Turkey, Cranberry sauce
Ham, Madiera sauce
Mashed Potatoes   Sweet Potatoes
Cauliflower   Stewed Tomatoes
Onion, sauce Béchamel Canned Corn

Lamb Chops with Peas
Chicken, sauté, a l'Espagnole
Baked Macaroni   Rice

Rock Punch

Broiled Golden Plover on Toast
Currant Jelly   Celery   Lettuce

Pudding, Souffle, a là Vanilla
Apple Pie   Cocoanut Pie
Chocolate Eclairs
CL's Foot Jelly
Assorted Cakes   Fruit Cake
Vanilla Ice Cream
Fruit   Cheese
Coffee

Hotel Ponce de Leon Spires

Hotel Ponce de Leon

Opening Menu
January 10, 1888

Blue Points

Blue point oysters were popular during this era. Found chiefly off Blue Point, Great South Bay, Long Island, New York, it was a feat to serve up such a delicacy far from their native habitat.

1 lb oysters
1/4 c cheddar cheese, grated
1 stick butter
2 oz sherry
1/4 c shallots, finely chopped
4 T flour
1/2 c mushrooms, thinly sliced
1 c cream
1/4 c parsley, chopped
salt and pepper to taste

Sauté shallots and mushrooms in butter until golden. Add oysters, salt, pepper, and sherry. Simmer for 5 minutes. Add flour to half a cup of cream, beat briskly with a fork and add to oyster mixture. Heat on low until blended and thickened. Spoon oyster sauce into individual baking bowls. Add cheese and parsley to other half cup of cream and heat until cheese is melted. Pour over oyster sauce in baking bowls and place in a preheated 350° oven for 10 minutes or until bubbly and lightly browned. Yields 4 servings.

Cream Soup, à la Reine
Consommé Printanière

4 c milk
1 c heavy cream
1/2 stick butter
1/3 c flour
1 t salt
1 c chicken stock
1/2 c dry sherry
1/4 t white pepper

In a large saucepan, melt butter. Blend in flour, stirring until smooth. Slowly stir in chicken stock and continue stirring until mixture is smooth. Simmer for 2 minutes. Add milk and cream and cook over very low heat, stirring constantly until thickened. Do not boil. Add sherry, salt, and pepper. Remove from heat and serve. Yields 6 servings.

Hors d'œuvres, Variés

Throughout St. Augustine's early years, formal entertainment was enjoyed by visiting royalty, high ranking government officials, and the town's upper class. However, regal entertainment reached its zenith when Henry Flagler opened his extravagant hotel juxtaposed against a background of natural beauty.

The Flagler grand hotels, first the Ponce de Leon, and then the Alcazar and Cordova, enticed the rich and the famous. Women wearing silk gowns designed and purchased in Paris and men wearing double-breasted suits and ascots combined to introduce an unparalleled elegance to the Ancient City, which was now being called the "Newport of the South."

St. Johns River Cocoanut Shrimp

1 lb med shrimp
1/2 c flour
1/2 t salt
1/2 t paprika
1/2 t pepper
2/3 c brandy
1 c coconut, grated
oil

Shell shrimp, leaving tails attached. Rinse and drain. Combine flour and spices, gradually stirring in brandy. Blend well. Place shrimp in batter. Heat 1" oil in heavy skillet. Remove shrimp from batter, dredge in coconut and fry in oil until coconut begins to brown. Remove and drain on paper. Serve hot or at room temperature with guava jelly and cream cheese. Yields 12-24 servings.

Hastings Eggplant Spread

1 lg eggplant
1/2 c olive oil
1 lg onion, chopped
2 tomatoes, peeled, chopped
1 green pepper, cored, chopped
salt and pepper to taste
1 clove garlic, minced
2 T white wine

Put a whole eggplant in a 400° oven and bake until soft, about 1 hour. Sauté onion, garlic, and pepper in oil until tender, but not brown. Peel and chop eggplant; mix with tomato. Add to sautéed seasoning. Add salt and pepper to taste. Add wine. Mix everything thoroughly and continue to cook gently until mixture is fairly thick. Cool, then place in refrigerator. Serve well chilled with thin slices of bread or crackers. Yields 2 cups.

Stuffed St. Augustine Sweet Onions

4 lg sweet onions
1/3 lb sausage, highly seasoned
1 c dressing, any type

Boil onions until soft. Cook sausage until very crumbly. Drain then add to dressing. When onions are cool, separate layers. Fill each "leaf" lengthwise with dressing, fold over and secure with a toothpick. Store in refrigerator until ready to serve. Run directly under broiler to brown and heat thoroughly. Yields 40-50.

The Ponce Cheese and Mushroom Balls

4 oz blue cheese, crumbled
1 T green onion, chopped
3 c fresh bread crumbs
1/4 t pepper
2 eggs, slightly beaten
1/4 c oil
1 c mushrooms, sliced

Combine cheese, 2 c bread crumbs, mushrooms, onion, pepper, and eggs in mixing bowl. Mix well. Let stand 10 minutes then shape into 1" balls. Roll cheese balls in remaining bread crumbs. Sauté cheese balls in oil until golden brown. Drain. Yields 2 dozen.

Avilés Spicy Meat Balls

1 lb ground beef or venison
1 t Worcestershire sauce
1/3 c onions, diced
6 oz datil pepper sauce
1/2 c bread crumbs
10 oz grape jelly
1/4 c oil

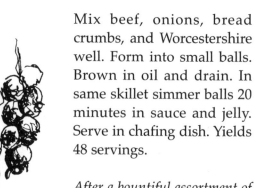

Mix beef, onions, bread crumbs, and Worcestershire well. Form into small balls. Brown in oil and drain. In same skillet simmer balls 20 minutes in sauce and jelly. Serve in chafing dish. Yields 48 servings.

After a bountiful assortment of appetizers, the waiters at the Ponce served the delectable, but somewhat filling third course, shrimp croquettes created by Chef Robert.

Broiled Shad

1-1/2 lbs shad, filleted, divided
1/2 lb shrimp, shelled
8 peppercorns
1 onion, sliced
1 bay leaf
1 T flour
1/8 t paprika
1/4 t nutmeg
3 T butter
1 egg, slightly beaten
1 c water
2 T datil pepper sauce
1 c sherry
1/2 c sour cream
1 T lemon juice
1/4 c heavy cream, whipped
1/2 c mushrooms, sliced
1/2 c feta cheese, crumbled
1/2 t salt

Croquettes of Shrimp, Robert

1 lb shrimp, shelled, diced
6 T butter
1 clove garlic, minced
2 eggs, beaten
8 T flour
2 T water
2 c milk
1 c cracker crumbs
salt and pepper to taste
1/4 c oil

Make cream sauce with butter, flour, and milk. Season with salt, pepper, and garlic. Add shrimp to cream sauce and refrigerate overnight. The next day, roll a tablespoon of the refrigerated mixture in cracker crumbs and mold to desired shape. A cone shape makes attractive croquettes. Combine eggs and water and dip croquettes into mixture. Roll again in crumbs. Fry in deep cooking oil (tested for hotness with a large bread crumb) until brown. Yields 4-6 servings.

The fourth course included shad fresh from the Atlantic Ocean and potatoes.

Melt 1 T butter in skillet. Add fillets then shrimp, water, sherry, lemon juice, salt, peppercorns, onion, and bay leaf. Bring to a boil, reduce heat and simmer gently for 6-8 minutes.

Carefully lift fillets from skillet, drain, and place in a well-buttered shallow baking dish. Drain shrimp and place on top of fish. Add mushrooms.

Melt remaining butter in small pan. Stir in flour, paprika, and nutmeg and cook until bubbly. Stir a little of the hot mixture into beaten egg then return this to the sauce. Stir over low heat until the mixture thickens, being careful not to boil. Fold in datil pepper sauce, sour cream, and whipped cream. Pour the sauce over the fish and shrimp. Sprinkle generously with cheese. Place in broiler about 5" from heat and brown lightly. Yields 6 servings.

Parisienne Potatoes

4 c potatoes, peeled, thinly sliced
1/4 t cayenne
3 T butter
1 c sharp cheese, grated
3 T flour
3/4 c green pepper, cored, chopped
1-1/2 c cream
1/2 c pimento, chopped
1 t salt

Melt butter and blend in flour. Slowly stir in cream. Add salt and cayenne and cook until smooth. Bring to a low boil, reduce heat, and add cheese. When melted, add green pepper, pimento, and spices. Fill a greased dish alternately with potatoes and sauce. Bake at 325° for 1 hour. Yields 8 servings.

And the foods kept coming, brought forth from the huge kitchens on mountainous platters covered with sterling silver domes. The fifth course consisted of beef, turkey, ham and madiera sauce, potatoes, and a variety of vegetables and starches.

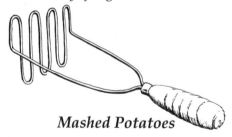

Mashed Potatoes

Potatoes:
2-1/2 lbs potatoes, peeled, diced
3 oz cream cheese, softened
1/2 c milk, heated
1 T horseradish
water

Mixture:
1/2 c green onions, sliced
2 cloves garlic, minced
3 T chicken broth
1 T pepper
1 t salt
1/4 c butter

Potatoes: Place potatoes in large saucepan and cover with water. Bring to a boil, reduce heat, and simmer 20 minutes or until potatoes are tender. Drain. In mixer, mash with remaining ingredients. Set aside.

Mixture: In skillet combine onions, garlic, spices, and butter and sauté until tender. Add broth, stir, then add mixture to potatoes. Beat until light and fluffy. Pour in greased dish and bake at 300° for 20 minutes. Yields 8 servings.

Onion, Sauce Béchamel

4 lg onions, thinly sliced
4 T butter
4 T flour
1/2 c milk
2 T dill
1 T parsley
1/4 t salt
1 t white pepper
1/2 c sour cream

In skillet melt butter then add onions and cook until translucent. Stir in flour and cook, stirring 1 minute. Gradually add milk and stir until smooth. Add remaining ingredients except cream and blend. Reduce heat and add cream. Heat thoroughly. Yields 4-6 servings.

As the famous and powerful guests finished their fifth course, the sixth was readied for its flourishing presentation, and included lamb, chicken, vegetables, and yet more starches.

Baked Macaroni

1 lb macaroni, cooked
1 lb sharp cheese, grated
1 c milk
1 t salt
1 T pepper
1 T paprika

Place macaroni in greased baking dish. Pour in milk. Sprinkle with salt and pepper. Top with cheese then sprinkle with paprika. Bake at 350° approximately 30 minutes or until cheese is brown and crunchy. Yields 6 servings.

Chicken, Sauté, a l'Espagnole

8 chicken breasts, skinned, deboned
1 t salt
1/2 t pepper
1/2 c butter
2 T lime juice
1/2 t dill weed
8 t scallions, tops on
6 oz feta cheese, crumbled

In baking dish arrange chicken then sprinkle with salt and pepper. In saucepan blend remaining ingredients except cheese. Pour over chicken. Top with cheese. Bake at 350° for 1 hour or until chicken is done. Yields 8 servings.

When each dish was emptied, it was deftly whisked away by white-gloved waiters standing at attention. Orchestra music drifted across the room, electric lights—still a rarity—twinkled in ornate chandeliers. Guests, such as the families of Henry Flagler's Standard Oil partners—the Rockefellers and the Wardens—and other notable families, the duPonts and the Carnegies, chatted while waiters filled crystal tumblers with rock punch.

Rock Punch

2 bottles champagne, chilled
2 c cranberry juice
2 orange rinds, grated
2 lemon rinds, grated
1/2 c light corn syrup
1 c brandy

Combine all ingredients. Serve over crushed ice. Yields 25 servings.

Let's leave the guests relaxing with their champagne and peek into the kitchen to learn what is involved in preparing such an elegant meal.

Our guide for this tour is the knowledge-able Anna M. Marcotte, editor of The Tatler.

Perhaps the first object to attract attention is the huge coffee boilers, where innumerable cups of coffee are made as by magic, and then a novel machine for washing dishes attracts attention; the plates are placed in a rack, the rack put into the machine and the very hot water dashed over them; when the rack is removed they dry themselves.

There are long tables with steam pipes beneath them where cooked food is kept hot, one person presiding over each. Beside them, great ovens where different kinds of bread are kept hot. Stacks of dishes ready for the waiters when needed. On the left is a large room well stocked with butter, bread and condiments, each waiter visiting the counter for his supply of these articles. Entering the kitchen there is directly in front of you a long line of ranges; at one fish is cooked, another beef, another lamb. At the end of the room are a number of copper boilers, holding perhaps a barrel; this is where the soups are made.

Beyond are the ice-boxes, really great rooms filled with meats, game and fowls, and a regular butcher in charge. A large range is particularly fitted up to bake griddle cakes, and one cook performs the work very deftly; near by is a toaster and beside it a large egg boiler.

continued next column . . .

In an adjoining room are the large ovens where at night the bread is baked and during the day cakes and pies; here as elsewhere everything was scrupulously clean; the cooks and their assistants wearing white caps and aprons were very pictur-esque. Below stairs were other storerooms equally orderly and appetizing.

In order to maintain the standards advertised in service, comfort, and especially, fine cuisine, the Ponce had to be managed by someone with a supreme talent for organizational skills. Charles W. Bixford was such a person.

Back from our brief tour of the well-equipped Ponce kitchen, let's watch while the eighth course is spread graciously before an admiring audience.

Broiled Golden Plover on Toast

A plover is a wading bird with a compact body, thick neck, short bill, and large eyes. Since plovers are migratory fowl and can no longer be hunted, substitute with chicken or duck.

4 plover breasts, deboned (use chicken or duck)
1/4 c onion, chopped
1 clove garlic, minced
1/2 t chili powder
1 T olive oil
1 lg tomato, crushed
1/4 c dry sherry
1/4 c water
2 T raisins
2 T pimiento-stuffed olives, sliced
1/2 t salt

1 t pepper
1/4 t oregano
1/8 t marjoram
1 bay leaf
4 t cornstarch
1 egg, boiled, chopped
6 slices hard bread, toasted

In a large kettle cook onion, garlic, and chili powder in oil until onion is tender but not brown. Stir in remaining ingredients except fowl, cornstarch, egg, and bread. Add breasts, turning once to coat. Cover and bake at 350° for 1 hour. Uncover and bake 15 minutes. Remove meat and set aside. Skim fat from juices, remove bay leaf, then measure out 1-1/2 c liquid (add a bit of water if needed). Discard remaining juices from kettle then return the 1-1/2 c liquid to the kettle. Blend in cornstarch and stir until thick. Place breasts back in the juice for 5 minutes, coating once. Remove plovers to bread slices then spoon sauce over each serving. Garnish with egg. Yields 4 servings.

The ninth and final course provided the guests with an amazing array of beautiful and delicious desserts.

Pudding, Souffle, a là Vanilla

2 eggs
1 c sugar
1 T vanilla
1/2 pt whipping cream, whipped
2 T flour
1 t baking powder
1 c pecans, chopped
butter

Beat eggs and sugar until light. Sift in flour and baking powder then add vanilla and pecans and stir well. Pour mixture into a buttered and floured 8" pan. Bake at 350° for approximately 10 minutes. Watch pudding carefully for when it rises and begins to brown, stir once then continue to bake. Bake 10 minutes longer or until lightly brown. Remove from oven and allow to cool. Top with cream. Yields 6 servings.

Apple Pie

Pie:
5 lg apples, cored, sliced
1/2 c brown sugar
2 T flour
1/2 t nutmeg
1/2 t cinnamon
2 T lemon juice
1 9" pastry shell, unbaked

Topping:
1/2 c brown sugar
1/2 c flour
1/2 c butter, sliced
1/2 c walnuts or pecans, chopped

Pie: Combine all ingredients and spoon into a pastry shell. Sprinkle with lemon juice.

Topping: Combine all ingredients except butter and sprinkle over apples. Top with butter. Bake at 400° for 45-55 minutes or until apples are tender. Cool. Yields 6 servings.

Cocoanut Pie

1-1/3 c coconut, grated
2 T butter
3 egg yolks
1/2 c cream
4 T sugar
3 T flour
1 c sugar
1 t vanilla
3 egg whites, stiffly beaten (add enough
  sugar to make stiff peaks)
1 pastry shell, unbaked

In saucepan simmer butter, sugar, flour, egg yolks, and cream until thick. Stir in 1 c coconut and vanilla. Cool then pour in pastry shell and top with egg whites. Sprinkle with remaining coconut. Bake at 325° approximately 20 minutes or until meringue is lightly browned. Yields 6 servings.

Chocolate Eclairs

Pastry:
2/3 c water
4 T butter
1 T sugar
1 c all-purpose flour, sifted
4 eggs

Filling:
1 c whipping cream, whipped
1/4 c sugar

Topping:
6 oz unsweetened chocolate, grated
4 T butter
2/3 c water, boiling
2 c sugar
4 T corn syrup
3 T brandy

Pastry: In a saucepan bring water, butter, and sugar to a boil. Remove from heat then add flour. Stir briskly until the mixture forms a hard ball. Add one egg at a time, beating rapidly. Drop by large spoonfuls onto a greased baking pan. In middle of oven bake at 450° for 5 minutes then turn oven to 350° and bake an additional 10-15 minutes or until pastry is brown and firm. Allow to cool. Split down middle but do not cut through to the bottom of the pastries.

Filling: Combine cream and sugar and whip until stiff. Spoon cream into each pastry.

Topping: In saucepan combine chocolate and butter. Stir until melted. Add remaining ingredients and blend well. Bring to a rapid boil and cook 5 minutes, stirring constantly. Cool slightly then ladle topping over pastries. Yields approximately 12 servings.

Orange Ice Box Cake

2 c milk
2 c orange juice
2 c sugar
2 T orange rind, grated
2 T cornstarch
2 c whipping cream, whipped
1 pkg gelatin & 2 T water
24 lady fingers, halved
4 eggs
1 orange, thinly sliced

Mix cornstarch and sugar, then add eggs. Scald milk in a double boiler and pour into mixture, blending well. Return mixture to double boiler and cook 10 minutes. Remove from heat. Dissolve gelatin in 2 T water. Add gelatin, orange juice, and rind to mixture. Cool. Fold in 1/2 of the cream. Line sides and bottom of spring form cake pan with lady fingers. Pour custard into pan. Refrigerate overnight. Prior to serving, remove from cake pan, placing upside down on serving plate. Pour remainder of cream over cake, then garnish with orange slices. Yields 10-12 servings.

Vanilla Ice Cream

3 cans condensed milk
1 can evaporated milk
1/2 pt whipping cream
3 qt milk
4 T vanilla
3 T lemon extract
1 box ice cream salt
2 bags ice

In ice cream churn container combine all ingredients except salt and ice and blend well. Secure churn blades then cover. Pour ice and salt in churn. Turn the crank until mixture is thick and creamy. Add ice and salt when ice begins to melt. Yields 4 quarts.

Henry Flagler was a self-made millionaire who left home at the early age of 14 with a few coins jingling in his pocket. The son of a Presbyterian minister, he was raised with a strong work ethic. Within several years he had secured a good job in Ohio. While there, he met another young man who had similar aspirations for success—John D. Rockefeller. They, together with Samuel Andrews and later William Warden and others, formed the Standard Oil Company.

Henry Flagler's wife, Mary, had been unhealthy for some time. During a particularly bitter New York winter, her doctor advised a visit to Florida in the hope that the warm climate might improve her health. After only a short time in St. Augustine and Jacksonville, business pressures required Henry Flagler to return to New York. Mary decided that she and their children would accompany him. Unfortunately, her health did not improve and she passed away in 1881.

After Mary's death, Henry Flagler returned to St. Augustine to "retire." However, with his extraordinary mind and his seemingly unlimited energy and financial resources, he soon saw business opportunities he wanted to pursue.

During his years in St. Augustine, he and his good friend, Dr. Andrew Anderson, attempted to urbanize the ancient city. Dr. Anderson had been named mayor and together the two men enthusiastically promoted development of the city and its infrastructure: paved roads, public utilities, and adequate fire and police protection. However, cautious city officials refused to grant a tax increase for such improvements. At his own expense, Henry Flagler

Hotel Alcazar

paved the streets surrounding his hotels and leading to his railway station. He constructed a building for municipal offices and, in 1888, donated funds toward the building of Alicia Hospital, named in honor of his second wife, Ida Alice.

In 1889, Henry Flagler began construction of Memorial Presbyterian Church at 36 Sevilla Street. It was built in memory of his daughter, Jennie Louise Flagler Benedict, who died enroute to St. Augustine. She was coming to stay with her father so that she might recuperate from the loss of her newborn daughter, Margery. The church was dedicated a year later and Jennie Louise, infant Margery, and Henry Flagler's beloved first wife, Mary, were interred in a tomb attached to the west side of the church. Ecumenical by nature, he also provided funds for land, construction, or remodeling of Grace Methodist Church at 8 Carrera Street; the Ancient City Baptist Church at 27 Seville Street; and the Catholic Cathedral facing the north side of the Plaza.

Within months of the opening of the Spanish Renaissance-style Ponce on what had been the site of Andrew Anderson's famous orange groves, Henry Flagler, an astute businessman, began construction of his second hotel, the Alcazar. It was described as having:

> . . . an interior court with a garden and fountains surrounded by open arcades, shops, and offices, and a large restaurant. Beyond are magnificent swimming baths . . . . Beyond the bath are courts for tennis and croquet . . . .
>
> A Handbook of Florida: Part I, 1890

For only $4.00 a day, an Alcazar guest would receive all of the above amenities as well as a spacious bedroom and private bath. Exceptional meals prepared by some of the world's finest chefs were available at an additional charge.

Henry Flagler was a brilliant host, envisioning the needs and desires of his clientele before they could express them. The

smallest of details preoccupied him. Each
meal was carefully planned, luxuriously
executed, and beautifully presented. The
hotel dining rooms offered only the finest
cuts of meat, the freshest seafood, and the
most succulent vegetables and fruits. To
control the quality of his produce, Henry
Flagler encouraged Thomas Hastings, a
relative of the architect of his hotels, to
farm land west of town near the St. Johns
River. The Flagler and Hastings joint venture supplied much of the produce that
the Flagler hotels required.

What Henry Flagler could not produce
on his own lands or those of his friends,
he imported. Fresh oranges, if not plucked
from the groves surrounding the Ponce
or in the Africa neighborhood, were
brought from the Halifax River near
present-day Ormond Beach, Florida.
Pineapples from the pineapple plantations
along the Indian River, near Cape
Canaveral, Florida, were also imported.

Seafood was caught daily including Spanish mackerel, shad, and drum. Shrimp
were netted in the Atlantic as well as the
St. Johns River. Oysters previously
shipped from New York, were now imported fresh from Cedar Key, a small island off the west coast of Florida. And diamondback terrapin turtle was harvested
from local brackish waters and tidal
streams.

Since the flyway for the redhead duck and
golden plover did not pass over Florida,
these migratory fowl were imported from
South America during the winter. Poultry, beef, and lamb were purchased in the
larger cities until Henry Flagler was as-
sured that St. Augustine's domesticated
animals had reached the stage of tender
perfection which he demanded for his dining tables.

MENU

THE ALCAZAR, 1889
DINNER

Cedar Key Oysters
Mock Turtle Soup, aux Quenelles
Consommé Printanieré Royale
Olives   Celery   Pickles   Radishes
Diamondback Terrapin,
a l'Alcazar, en Caisses
Spanish Mackerel broiled,
Maitre d'Hotel
Potatoes Parisiennes Iced Cucumbers
Boiled Corned Beef Brisket,
new Cabbage
Fillet of Beef, larded a la Catalina
Sweetbreads braised au Salpicón
Cream Fritters, Sauce Chartreuse
Roast Philadelphia Chicken,
stuffed, Giblet Gravy
Fresh String Beans Buttered Beets
Rice   Fried Egg Plant
Boiled, Mashed and Sweet Potatoes
Punch Martini
Fried Hominy
Red-head Duck, roasted, Quince Jelly
Tomato Salad
Messina Pudding, Port Wine Sauce
Plum Pie   Almond Tartelettes
Cocoanut Pie   Bisque Glacé
Champagne Jelly
Tutti Fruitti Ice Cream
Fancy Cakes, Assorted
Halifax River Oranges
Almeira Grapes
Indian River Pineapples
Cluster Raisins
Strawberries with Cream
Assorted Nuts
Brie and American Cheese Crackers
Coffee

Alcazar Menu
1889

Cedar Key Oysters

9 doz (3 pts) oysters, shucked
1/2 t red pepper
1 sm bell pepper, cored, chopped
1/2 t black pepper
1 lg onion, finely chopped
1 T Worcestershire sauce
3 cloves garlic, finely chopped
juice of 1 lemon
1/2 loaf French bread, thinly sliced
1 rib celery, finely chopped
2 eggs
1 stick butter
1/2 c milk
1 t salt
1/2 c parsley, chopped
1/2 t dried mustard
1/2 c green onion tops, chopped

In large skillet sauté onion, bell pepper, garlic, and celery in butter. Grind oysters on large blade in meat grinder and add to skillet. Add seasonings and bring to boil. Remove from heat and cool. Toast bread, crumble, then add to oyster mixture. Beat eggs in milk and add to oyster mixture. Mix

in parsley and onion tops. Place in chafing dish and serve with assorted crackers. Yields 30-40 servings.

Mock Turtle Soup,
aux Quenelles

Quenelles are light fish dumplings. Since they are somewhat tricky to make, be sure to have all ingredients ready in advance.

Quenelles:
1 lb fish, filleted
2 egg whites
2 t salt
1/4 t pepper
1/4 t nutmeg
2 c heavy cream
1/2 c parsley

Liquid for cooking quenelles:
1 t tarragon
8 peppercorns
1 bay leaf
1 onion
1 c white wine

Soup:
3 lbs fish, filleted
6 c water
2 c milk
1/4 lb butter
1 T flour
1 c cream
1/2 t mace
2 eggs, hard boiled, diced
1/2 t dry mustard

Quenelles: Cut fish into small pieces. Add egg and all seasonings except parsley. Grind until smooth. Keeping mixture in grinder, place in refrigerator and chill 1 hour. Remove and while grinding, gradually pour in cream. Add parsley. Mixture can stay in refrigerator for several days until ready to use.

Cooking quenelles: Simmer ingredients in large pot for 1 hour. Remove quenelles mixture from refrigerator. Carefully drop mixture by large spoonfuls into hot liquid. Cover pot and cook until firm. Drain.

Soup: Boil fish and water until 4 c of liquid remains. Add milk and butter. Remove fish, allow to cool, grind, and then return to broth. Let broth cook down a bit more. Dissolve flour and seasonings in cream then add to broth. Stir in eggs. Prior to serving place 2 quenelles in a bowl. Pour soup over and serve. Yields 8-10 servings.

Spanish Mackerel broiled, Maitre d'Hotel

1 mackerel, halved
salt and pepper to taste
1 t paprika
1/2 c feta cheese
4 T lemon juice
1/2 c white wine
1/2 stick butter

Brown butter in large baking dish. Salt and pepper fish and place skin side up in dish. Add wine. Bake at 400° for 15 minutes. Turn fish and sprinkle with lemon juice. Bake 5 minutes longer. Sprinkle paprika and cheese on fish then place under broiler until brown. Yields 2 servings.

Fillet of Beef, larded a la Catalina

8 oz beef sirloin, thinly sliced
1/2 t salt
3 lg onions, thinly sliced
2 T rum
1/2 t sugar
5 T oil
1/2 c wine
1 T cornstarch

Mix beef with rum, wine, 2 T oil, cornstarch, sugar, and salt, and marinate for 1 hour. Reserve liquid. Heat 3 T oil in skillet and sauté meat until slightly brown. Add onions and continue to brown on low. Pour reserved liquid on top and heat. Yields 4 servings.

Sweetbreads braised au Salpicón

Sweetbread is traditionally made from the thymus gland of young animals, particularly calves and lambs. This recipe uses beef and mushrooms instead.

1 lb roast beef, cooked, shredded
2 eggs, beaten
2 c bread crumbs
1 T parsley
1 T salt
1 T pepper
1 T chives
1 T thyme
1 c mushrooms, thinly sliced
4 T onion, minced
1/2 c brandy

In large bowl, combine all ingredients, except mushrooms and brandy, and stir well. Place mixture in a well greased baking dish and bake at 350° until brown. Warm brandy and add mushrooms and cook until tender. Spoon over sweetbreads. Yields 6 servings.

Cream Fritters, Sauce Chartreuse

1 c cornmeal
1/2 c buttermilk
1/2 c water
1/2 c flour
1 T sugar
1 t salt
1 t baking powder
1 t bacon drippings
1/2 c spring onions, thinly sliced
1 c heavy cream
2 T parsley
2 c oil

Mix together all ingredients except cream, onions, and oil. Heat oil in iron skillet until very hot. Drop fritter mixture by teaspoons in hot fat and brown. Remove and drain. In saucepan, heat cream and onions and pour over fritters. Sprinkle fritters with additional parsley. Yields 6 servings.

Punch Martini

6 c lemonade
4-1/2 oz grenadine
16 c orange juice
6 c pineapple juice
1 bottle gin
1 bottle vodka
1 bottle dry vermouth

Mix well. Pour over ice in large serving bowl. Yields 100 servings.

Street Scene

As empty bone china dishes are removed and crystal goblets filled with Punch Martini, let's slip outside the Alcazar to take a brief stroll about the Plaza before the next course is served.

The nearby streets are dirt and there are few large trees left after the area was cleared for development. Gone are most of the acclaimed Anderson orange trees. Henry Flagler's magnificent Hotel Ponce de Leon faces the Alcazar. Just to the right is the Cordova Hotel. Lights twinkle from hotel windows as polite conversation, tinkling glass, strains of classical music, and muted laughter drift across the Alcazar courtyard.

The clip-clop of horse hooves approach. The St. Augustine Transfer Company sends its omnibuses and phaetons to the hotels to wait for the northern "strangers" who wish to take an evening ride along the bayfront. The hack drivers, Freedmen from the community of Africa, wave as strollers pass.

Shopkeepers have locked their doors and headed home, a few townspeople are visiting friends and neighbors, and several stray dogs roam the Plaza. Most of the people in St. Augustine are at home planning their next day and deciding how they will meet the needs of their families while guests dining in palatial surroundings enjoy their meal.

Now, let's tiptoe quickly back into the Alcazar as the remainder of the chef's creations are presented.

Fried Hominy

Hominy is a southern dish made from hulled corn ground into particles. Its more familiar name is "grits."

2 lbs hominy, cooked
6 strips bacon, cut into pieces
1/8 t pepper
2 scallions with tops, thinly sliced
1/2 t salt

Fry bacon in a large, heavy skillet until brown and crisp. Add hominy and salt, stirring for 5 minutes. Add pepper and scallions. Stir an additional 5 minutes. Yields 6-8 servings.

Red-head Duck, roasted, Quince Jelly

2 ducks, prepared
2 onions
1 c sherry
salt and pepper
2 strips bacon
1 c quince jelly

Preheat oven to 375°. Season ducks inside and out with salt and pepper. Wrap each onion with a piece of bacon and place in cavity of duck. Put ducks in roaster and pour sherry on top of each. Cook for 2 hours, basting frequently. Serve with quince jelly. Yields 2-4 servings.

Plum Pie

Filling:
1 c beef suet, chopped
1 c almonds, blanched, sliced
1 c and 2 T brown sugar
1-1/4 c flour, all-purpose, sifted
1/2 c milk
1 t baking soda
2 eggs, well beaten
1 t salt

1 c currants
1/2 t nutmeg
1 c plums, seeded
1/4 t mace
1 t cinnamon
1/2 c brandy
1 c bread crumbs, soft

Topping:
6 T butter, softened
1-1/2 t vanilla
1-1/2 c powdered sugar
sherry to taste

Filling: Combine suet, sugar, milk, and eggs. Mix fruits and almonds with 1/4 c of flour. Sift remaining flour with soda, salt, and spices. Add fruits, crumbs, flour, and spice mixture to suet mixture. Mix well. Turn into well greased 2 qt covered pudding mold. Steam 3 hours with water 1/2 depth of mold, replenishing water during steaming to keep proper depth. Turn out on platter. Heat brandy in pan then pour over pudding. Light brandy and when fire subsides, add topping.

Topping: Cream butter well. Add sugar gradually then vanilla and sherry. Yields 6-8 servings.

Almond Tartlettes

Crust:
3 oz cream cheese, softened
1/2 c butter, softened
1 c plain flour, sifted

Custard:
1 egg
1 t vanilla
3/4 c light brown sugar
2/3 c almonds, chopped
1 T butter, softened

Crust: Cream butter and cheese. Stir in flour. Chill 1 hour then shape into 2 dozen round dough balls. Press in ungreased miniature muffin tins. Fill with custard.

Custard: Mix egg, sugar, butter, and vanilla. Sprinkle nuts in bottom of crust. Pour custard over nuts. Bake 20-25 minutes at 300°. Yields 2 dozen.

Tutti Fruitti Ice Cream

Tutti Fruitti was the term given to a popular Victorian dessert which contains a variety of chopped candied fruits.

4 eggs, beaten
2 c sugar
4 c milk
2 c cream
2 T flour
1/2 t vanilla
1 c candied fruits, assorted, chopped

Combine all ingredients and freeze. Yields 12 servings.

Brie Cheese

5 lbs Brie cheese
1 c dill
1 c currants, dried
1 c almonds, slivered
1 c walnuts, finely chopped
1/2 c poppy seeds

The Capo Bath House

Carefully cut away the rind from the top of the Brie. Using the back of the knife, lightly mark the top into 10 equal wedge-shaped areas. Sprinkle half of the currants onto one of the wedge-shaped areas and press gently into surface. Repeat procedure with half of the walnuts, dill, poppy seeds, and almonds, patting each garnish with the wedge-shaped areas as you proceed around the top. Wrap and refrigerate for no more than 4 hours. Allow to stand at room temperature 30 minutes before serving. Serve with crackers and fresh fruit. Yields 20-30 servings.

Filling the stomachs of the northern "strangers" was a serious enough task for St. Augustine's innkeepers, but filling the holiday time of the idle rich was an equally important challenge. If Henry Flagler's guests became bored with hotel food, he'd hire boats to ferry them across North River to North Beach. There they'd swim and picnic on oysters roasted by the Usina or the Capo families. Served with oysters were chicken perlo, Minorcan clam chowder, corn-dodgers, and steamed corn-on-the-cob—all for only 25¢ a person.

Hotel managers would also arrange a cakewalk for the guests, or offer them croquet on the lawn or golf in the shadows of *crumbling old Fort Marion. The more adventuresome tourists fished or sailed on the Matanzas River. Others took the horse-drawn railway car across the bay and marshland to Anastasia Island to climb the Lighthouse, visit the Alligator Farm, or collect seashells at South Beach. Restless strangers also had the choice of simply strolling along the bayfront, swimming at the round Capo Bath House at the foot of present-day Cathedral Place, or joining the St. Augustine Yacht Club located next door. Wandering the narrow streets of the ancient Spanish town was always a favorite pastime.*

A stylish competitor, the Casa Monica, opened near the Hotel Ponce de Leon, on January 17, 1888, one week after the Ponce. Named for St. Augustine's mother, the Casa Monica's dining room was described as:

> . . . one of the handsomest in the country . . . . The tables . . . laid with handsome damask, beautiful china and silver . . . forming a picture suggestive of feasts and banquets.
>
> The Tatler, 1888

Henry Flagler rapidly engulfed his competitor. He purchased the Casa Monica the following year and changed its name to the Cordova, the street which it faced. He then connected the Cordova with the Alcazar by a second-story walkway across Cordova Street. With this purchase, Henry Flagler created a monopoly of courtly hotels for Northern high society. Harper's New Monthly Magazine, in March 1893, advertised this triumvirate:

> . . . [With] the Flagler group of St. Augustine hotels . . . cost is not uppermost in the minds of those who spend much time in them. I know of no place, public or private, where the power of wealth so impresses itself upon the mind as at this group of Florida hotels. It is not because the owner's constant presence brings millions to mind, or that he is known to have made his own way, and is said to have brought his dinner to his office with him every day until he was worth a million. It is the spot itself—the finding of a group of palaces in such strong contrast with all the rest in Florida. It is the change from a field where the other charms are all natural to a mass of beauties that are made by hand.

The sheer magnitude of dreaming, designing, and then developing such magnificent hotels was an overwhelming feat even for Henry Flagler. In addition, in 1893, he built a 15 room winter estate for his second wife, Ida Alice. It was located on Valencia Street adjacent to Memorial Presbyterian Church and aptly named Kirkside, meaning "beside the church." The mansion no longer stands, having been demolished in 1950.

Henry Flagler continued to build his railway and hotel empire. He pushed the Florida East Coast Railway south to Palm Beach in 1894. There he created the magnificent Royal Poinciana and Breakers Hotels, an oceanside community, and a town for his workers in nearby West Palm Beach.

He then extended the railway south to the small community of Fort Dallas, soon to be known as Miami. He built a terminal station, railway yards, laid out streets in the proposed town, and built a grand hotel, the Royal Palm.

While Henry Flagler continued to build his railway to the southern tip of Florida, additional hotels were being constructed in the "Newport of the South." Henry Flagler's remarkable three had created such a magnetic attraction to the nation's oldest city that entrepreneurs attempted to emulate his success. When the winter winds blew down from the Arctic, newspapers and national magazines carried numerous advertisements and articles featuring the fine hostelries opened during the winter season in sunny St. Augustine. Each hotel announced its grand opening for the season and each was distinguished in its decor, culinary achievements, and comfort. Since St. Augustine's tourist season coincided with northern winters, it ran from December to April. By 1900 the town boasted more than a dozen hotels. The St. Augustine Hotel burned in 1887 when its boiler exploded, engulfing the building in flames. The San Marco was destroyed by fire in 1897.

Both the Florida House and the Magnolia remained favorite hostelries until destroyed by fire; the Florida House in 1914, the Magnolia in 1926. Other hotels built for the more modestly inclined included the Granada and the Buckingham, neighbors to Flagler's three. New hotels which faced the Matanzas River were the Ocean View, the Marion, and the Monson: the Monson destroyed during the same fire that demolished the Magnolia; the Ocean View razed in the 1960s.

Throughout the Gilded Age of Henry Flagler and the golden years of St. Augustine's tourist trade, each hotel was always filled to capacity during the season.

When Henry Flagler decided to promote St. Augustine as the "Newport of the South," a friend asked him why he chose that area. Displaying no humility, he responded:

> I believe this State is the easiest place for many men to gain a living. I do not believe anyone else will develop it if I do not.
> Henry Flagler, 1885

Throughout the 1890s Henry Flagler had personal problems. His second wife, Ida Alice, had been mentally ill for years. By 1897 her condition had deteriorated to the extent that she was placed in a private institution. Although they never saw each other again, Henry Flagler provided generously for her care. When she died 33 years later, her trust fund was valued at over $15 million.

In April, 1901, the Florida State Legislature passed a bill which made insanity grounds for divorce. A few months later, Henry Flagler filed for divorce from Ida Alice. In August the divorce was granted and he married Mary Lily Kenan of Kenansville, North Carolina, whom he had met years earlier in St. Augustine.

After their wedding, the couple moved to Palm Beach where he built the magnificent Whitehall, now the Flagler Museum, as a wedding gift for Mary Lily. The Flaglers used Whitehall as their winter home for the next decade. During that period, he undertook his most controversial accomplishment—the Overseas Extension of the Florida East Coast Railway to Key West. It was completed on January 22, 1912.

Eighteen months later, on May 20, 1913, Henry Flagler died. By his request, he was brought back to his first Florida home—St. Augustine.

On May 23, 1913, under a canopy of dismal clouds, a Florida East Coast Railway train pulled into the St. Augustine station, a lone whistle announcing its arrival. While trains across Florida stood still in silent tribute, Henry Flagler's coffin was lifted from his private rail car and placed in a waiting Landau. Two black stallions pulled the funeral carriage down a street Henry Flagler had paved. Thousands lined the route in solemn respect. The funeral procession proceeded to his first hotel, the magnificent Ponce de Leon, where he lay in state under the great rotunda. Promptly at 3 PM, the cortege continued one block west to Memorial Presbyterian Church, where Henry Morrison Flagler was laid to rest beside Mary, Jennie Louise, and Margery.

*Top to bottom:
Janie Young Price
House,
Lincolnville;
St. Francis Inn;
Oldest Wooden
School House
Museum*

Chapter VIII.
Restoration and Rehabilitation
1913-1964

> *St. Augustine has fallen into a gentle and wholly delightful*
> *shabbiness since the passing of its climax of prosperity.*
> Old Seaport Towns of the South, *1917*

*I*n 1917, when *Old Seaport Towns of the South* was published, there was some truth to its description of St. Augustine. Henry Flagler was gone and, with his death, something had been irrevocably lost in St. Augustine. Was it style? Was it allure? Or was it simply that the environment which brought Flagler and the affluent to St. Augustine had changed?

Whatever the reason, St. Augustinians persevered. The years from 1913 through the end of World War I were a transitional time for the city. Anna Marcotte, owner of *The Tatler*, expressed her frustrations as she watched in dismay the continued lethargy of city officials. Once she had reported on the banquets and balls at Henry Flagler's hotels during the Gilded Age; now she publicly berated community leaders for their obvious apathy.

> *St. Augustine must wake to the fact that she is a resort, that if*
> *she is not to sink to a village of a few inhabitants, she must*
> *stay in the race, grow in cleanliness and beauty, or sit down*
> *and see her visitors of former years pass . . . by on their journey*
> *to even newer, more progressive resorts.*
> The Tatler, *1914*

By 1915, St. Augustine's population was 4,000, double what it had been when Henry Flagler arrived in the mid-1880s. City officials finally heeded advice from *The Tatler*, from Dr. Andrew Anderson, and from others, and initiated improvements in St. Augustine's infrastructure—including the paving of roads.

The invention of the gasoline operated automobile in the mid-1910s brought the necessity for roadbuilding to the forefront. The county appropriated $650,000 to brick 65 miles of road, part of which remains today and is dubbed the "old brick road."

Better roads brought more cars to the area. In fact, one group of men intent on justifying a new road through St. Johns County counted the cars. In November of 1915 over 1,000 cars passed through the county heading either north or south.

The advent of the automobile brought increased tourism which increased the need for convenient, inexpensive sleeping accommodations near roadways. Those practical forerunners of modern-day motels were called auto camps or motor or tourist courts.

Travelers heading south during the winter months who brought their own camping gear or attached camper devices to their Model-T's were nicknamed "tin can tourists." They ate from tin cans, lived in tin cans (the forerunner of the domed camper), and spent very little "tin" money. Those thrifty tourists were the harbingers of visitors who would soon arrive in such numbers that collectively they changed the state's economy.

Even the movie industry rolled into St. Augustine, using many of the city's unique and historical buildings as backdrops for their productions.

Small diners were built along St. Augustine's new roads to provide travelers with home-cooked meals. In order to meet the needs of Florida's expanding tourist industry, many Florida Crackers turned from plowing and ranching to road building and construction. And many a housewife abandoned her kitchen to fry eggs and bacon at the local diner.

During the period from 1913 to 1964, a wider variety of foods became available as trade with foreign countries expanded. Spice selections increased.

The supermarket replaced the corner grocery store. More instant foods lined grocery shelves and frozen dinners filled freezers. After the 1950s, previously hand-selected meats cut especially for a customer were replaced with pre-cut selections. Family gardens, jelly making, and canning began to disappear as women left their homes to seek outside employment.

Electric and gas ranges replaced wood-burning stoves. Electric refrigerators replaced iceboxes. After World War II, kitchen technology rapidly improved ranges, refrigerators, mixers, mashers,

grinders, and graters. Pyrex, Melmac, and Corning Ware were born. The dishwasher was invented! Plastic eating utensils and styrofoam plates ushered in the "throw away" era. These paper and plastic food containers then advanced the growth of the fast food industry.

In the 1920s, St. Augustine built its first ice plant. Freezers were improved for home use, preservatives were added to commercial foods to lengthen shelf life, and plastic wrap and aluminum foil became widely available.

Surprisingly, World War I did not discourage tourism. Since travel abroad for the wealthy was impossible while battles in Europe raged, the years between 1914 and 1919 found more and more visitors wintering at the three Flagler hotels, as well as at the smaller hostelries and boarding houses operating in and near the town. Increased tourism created a need for better services for guests.

During the First World War years, Florida became the training ground for thousands of soldiers as its climate and wooded areas were conducive to outdoor instruction. The state's warm weather also enabled it to become a major supplier of produce for the military. Increased demand for farm products created a rise in farm prices which in turn generated additional revenue in the Hastings-St. Augustine area. And although there was a slight food shortage during the war, overall St. Augustinians suffered very little.

By 1920, St. Augustine's population had reached 6,000. Military personnel who had trained in Florida during the war found the region so much to their liking that they returned at war's end, bought land, and built homes. This contributed to the great Florida Land Boom which continued until 1926 when land prices dropped and businesses failed. The end of Florida's bullish decade was connected to the economic disaster which engulfed the United States in 1929.

However, what hurt the nation had relatively little impact on St. Augustine. Tourists from southern states crossed the Florida state line to spend their few dollars along the sandy shores of St. Augustine's pristine beaches. They delighted in shell collecting, modest sunbathing, and touring the antiquated Spanish town.

The Florida summer tourists season officially began in Florida, oddly enough, with the advent of the Great Depression. As the dust bowl blew heavily across the Midwest and bread lines lengthened in the north, Florida inched its way, ever so slowly, toward strengthening what would become its most important economic base—tourism.

It was during this period that Dr. Andrew Anderson decided St. Augustine needed monuments. Within a few years, he placed a marble fountain in the Plaza (only its base remains today), and donated the imposing statue of Ponce de León which stands guard at the east end of the Plaza. He also commissioned the sculpting of noble lions to rest at the foot of a new concrete and steel bridge crossing the Matanzas River. The bridge was later named the Bridge of Lions.

By 1930, St. Augustine's population was 12,000. The decade ushered in an important, but almost forgotten concept—restoration. The Oldest House and Fort Marion were preserved, with the Fort becoming a National Monument in 1924. In 1942 its original name Castillo de San Marcos was restored.

However, much of St. Augustine's culturally and historically important buildings were in need of repair. Largely due to the efforts of Albert Manucy, a Minorcan and professional historian, as well as many others, federal funds and private donations were secured to preserve many of the city's historical public structures. At the same time, committed individuals and organizations worked to save and restore a number of other beautiful historical properties.

St. Francis Inn

Gaspar Garcia House, c. 1791
Established as an Inn in 1845
Remodeled in 1930
Named the St. Francis Inn, 1948
279 St. George Street

The St. Francis Inn was built of native coquina during the Second Spanish Period. It served as a residence until about 1845 when it was turned into a boarding house by Sara and Anna Dummett. When Sara married the Civil War General, William J. Hardee, also a St. Augustinian, the property transferred to him. Although feelings remained strained for some time between townspeople and tourists before, during, and after the Civil War, the Inn continued to do a good business throughout the 19th century, operating under a variety of proprietors and names. The St. Francis Inn remains the oldest and most historic of the city's comfortable vacation spots for "strangers."

Sara Dummett's Apple Butter

2 c apple juice
12-14 apples, preferably Jonathan or Winesap, cored, quartered
1-1/4 t orange zest (zest is the rind)
sugar
cinnamon
allspice
cloves
1/2 c Chablis
oil

Combine apples and apple juice in lightly oiled stock pot. Cover and cook on low for 2-3 hours. When fruit is tender, put through a food mill to remove peel. Measure cooked fruit and return to stock pot. For each pint of sieved cooked fruit, add 1 c sugar, 1 t cinnamon, 1/2 t allspice, 1/2 t cloves, and orange zest. Stir well. Cover and cook on high for 1 hour. Remove cover and add Chablis then simmer another 1-1/2 hours. Spoon into sterilized jars. Yields approximately 6 pints.

St. Francis Inn Bread Pudding

Pudding:
1-1/2 c milk
1 loaf bread (or use leftover muffins, rolls, etc.) cut in 2" pieces
1/2 c sugar
3 t cinnamon
2 t vanilla
1 t almond
1 c pecan pieces

8 eggs, beaten
2 c apples, diced
1 banana, diced
sprinkle of brown sugar
1/2 c butter, melted

Caramel Sauce:
1 c brown sugar
1/2 c water
few drops lemon juice

Pudding: Combine bread and milk making sure all the bread is wet. Mix in remaining pudding ingredients, except brown sugar and butter. Put half of batter in a 2 qt baking dish. Cover with brown sugar and 1/4 c butter. Add remaining batter and cover with remaining brown sugar and butter. Bake at 350" for 1-1/2 hours.

Caramel Sauce: In saucepan combine ingredients and cook on low until caramel colored. Pour over pudding mixture. Yields 6-8 servings.

King's Bakery, c. 1770
Restored 1934
97 Marine Street

Located within feet of the St. Francis Barracks, the King's Bakery was built to supply fresh bread for the British military. At various times it was also used as a storehouse for flour and as a military hospital.

The King's Bakery holds the distinction of being the last remaining building from the British occupation of St. Augustine. It was remodeled in 1934 by the Florida National Guard Foundation.

Sour Dough Bread

Starter:
1 c flour
1 c milk
1/2 c sugar

Bread:
6 c bread flour, unsifted
1/2 c sugar
1/2 c oil
1 T salt
1-1/2 c water, warmed
1 c sour dough starter (from above)
1/4 c butter, melted

Starter: Combine all ingredients, cover, shake, and leave for several days. Do not use same day it is made. Never let starter get down to less than 1 cup. As the starter is reduced by using, add to it by combining all of the above starter ingredients. This is called "feeding" the starter.

Bread: In a large bowl mix flour, sugar, and salt. Stir in water, oil, and starter and mix, making a stiff batter. Push dough aside in bowl and wipe bowl with oil. Turn dough over to grease all sides. Cover and let stand in a warm place overnight. Next morning punch down dough and knead a little using a small amount of extra flour if needed. Place in greased bread pans. Brush lightly with oil. Let rise all day and night, approximately 10-12 hours. Bake on the bottom rack at 350° for 30-45 minutes. Remove and brush with melted butter. Yields 2 loaves.

Juan Esteban de Peña House
c. 1740
Restored in 1932 as the
Peña-Peck House Museum
143 St. George Street

The Peña-Peck House, now the Woman's Exchange, is one of St. Augustine's original colonial buildings, dating from the First Spanish Period. Built of native coquina, it was the home of the Royal Spanish Treasurer, Juan Esteban de Peña.

During the British Period it was the town house of Lieutenant Governor John Moultrie who also owned the plantation, Bella Vista, near present-day Moultrie Creek. At the beginning of the American Territorial Period in 1821, it was used to house slaves.

In 1835 the house was purchased by Dr. Seth Peck, a native of Connecticut. Dr. Peck restored the house, adding a second story of wood frame construction. The first floor housed his medical offices and a general store while he and his family occupied the second floor. In 1841 Dr. Peck died during a yellow fever epidemic and the house was deeded to his wife, Sarah.

Daughter Lucy married George Burt and their four children were born in the Peck house. In 1931, Anna, Lucy and George's only child to live to adulthood, willed the house to St. Augustine. Since the city was having financial difficulties, the Woman's Exchange took over the house to honor its longtime member, Anna. On May 5, 1932, the house was opened to the public. It is filled with Peck family treasures, including magnificent 18th century furniture from Sarah Peck's dowry.

The Woman's Exchange continues to maintain the house and shop. In addition, it caters dinners for groups and sponsors a popular spring luncheon series featuring favorite recipes.

Anna's Chicken

6 chicken breasts, split
2 t paprika
2 c sour cream
2 cloves garlic
1/4 t lemon juice
4 t salt
4 t Worcestershire sauce
dash pepper
4 t celery salt
1/2 c butter, melted
bread crumbs

Marinate chicken overnight in all ingredients except butter and bread crumbs. Next day roll each piece in bread crumbs and place in a single layer baking pan. Baste every 15 minutes with melted butter. Bake at 350° for 1 hour. Yields 6 servings.

Peña-Peck Hot Chicken Salad

3 c chicken, cooked, diced
1/2 can chicken soup
2 c celery, thinly sliced
1/2 c almonds, slivered
2 T lemon juice
2 T pimiento, chopped
2 T onion, diced
1/2 c green pepper, cored, diced
1/2 c mild cheese, grated
1/2 c mayonnaise
3 c potato chips, finely crushed

Mix all ingredients except cheese and potato chips. Place in a greased casserole dish then sprinkle with cheese and chips. Bake at 350° for 45 minutes. Yields 6 servings.

Dr. Peck's Favorite Rum Rolls

2 pkgs soft rolls
1/2 c butter, melted
1/3 c sugar
2 T rum

Stir in sugar, butter, and rum. Perforate rolls using fork. Spread on rolls. Bake 15 minutes at 350°. Yields approximately 2 dozen.

Clarissa Anderson Gibbs' Huguenot Torte

2 eggs
1 t vanilla
1/2 c sugar
4 T flour
1/2 t salt
2-1/2 t baking powder
1 c pecans, chopped
1 t almond extract
1 c heavy cream
2 c apples, diced

Beat eggs and salt until light and fluffy. Gradually beat in sugar. Fold in apples and pecans. Add flavorings and flour mixed with baking powder. Pour into well-greased pan about 8 x 8 x 2". Place on cookie sheet to protect oven rack as torte will swell up and ooze over the edge.

If torte swells prick with a fork. Bake for 45 minutes at 325°. May be eaten warm, but best chilled and then topped with whipped cream. Yields 4-6 servings.

Andrew and Juana Ximenez House, c. 1798
Ximenez-Fatio House Museum, 1939
20 Avilés Street

Located in the heart of the original boundaries of the Spanish colonial settlement, the Ximenez house was constructed of coquina block with tabby floors and the typical detached coquina kitchen of the period. During the late 1790s the owner maintained a store on the ground floor with living quarters above.

From 1830 until 1875 it was a first rate boarding house for strangers from the north. Its last innkeeper was Louisa Fatio.

The Ximenez-Fatio House is one of the few structures remaining in St. Augustine from the Second Spanish Period. Purchased in 1939 by the Florida Society of Colonial Dames of America, it was authentically restored and refurnished and is listed on the National Register of Historic Places.

Colonial Dames Lemon Sticks

Batter:
1/2 c butter
1/2 c powdered sugar
2 egg yolks
1 c flour
2 t lemon rind, grated

Meringue topping:
2 egg whites, beaten stiff
1/2 c powdered sugar
1 T lemon juice
1/2 c pecans, chopped

Batter: Cream butter and add sugar gradually. Lightly beat egg yolks and add to mixture. Stir in flour and rind and mix until smooth. Spread evenly in bottom of ungreased 9 x 13" pan. Bake 10 minutes at 350°.

Topping: Gradually add sugar to beaten egg whites. Add lemon juice and fold in pecans. Spread meringue over baked layer and bake 25 minutes longer. Cool then cut into 1 x 3" sticks. Yields 32 sticks.

Ximenez-Fatio House Orange Glazed Nuts

1-1/2 c sugar
1/2 c water
2 oranges, juice
2 oranges, rind, finely grated
1 lb pecan halves
pinch of salt

Combine sugar and water in a heavy saucepan. Cook until it forms a soft ball when a half teaspoon is dropped in cold water. Add rind and juice, salt, and nuts. Stir until well coated. When opaque, spread on wax paper and separate. When glaze is hard, store in air-tight tin. Yields 24 servings.

Seville Orange Marmalade

Marmalades are bits of fruit and peel cooked to a translucent stage in a heavy syrup. Patience and careful stirring are necessary so that thickening without scorching can be achieved.

6 Seville oranges
water according to measure
5 lbs sugar

Select blemish-free oranges and wash thoroughly. Grate skin lightly to release bitter oils. Cut oranges into quarters and remove seeds. Grind in food chopper. Measure fruit. Add twice as much water as fruit into a stainless steel or plastic container of sufficient size. Let stand overnight. Next day place mixture in deep, heavy cooker to boil until peel is tender, about 1 hour. Let cool to measure quantity. For every cup of fruit and juice, add 3/4 c sugar. Boil marmalade until the juice thickens and forms a jelly when tested after 15 minutes of cooking. Ladle into sterile 1/2 pt canning jars and process in water bath 10 minutes. Yields about 16 1/2 pt jars.

Juan Genopoly House, c. 1805
Restored in 1939 as the
Oldest Wooden School House
Museum
14 St. George Street

Built by Juan Genopoly, this building is the only wooden structure remaining from the Second Spanish Period. Genopoly, a Minorcan from the ill-fated colony of New Smyrna, Florida, was an enterprising individual. He purchased land north of the fort for growing crops which he sold from his home. He also owned a prosperous dairy farm and supplied milk for many of the city's residents.

The house remained a residence throughout the 19th century while at the same time being advertised as "The Old School House." Early records indicate that a small school operated from the house around 1811 and again after the Civil War. In 1920, it became a tea house and in 1924-1925 was a restaurant.

In 1939 the Genopoly House was restored by Walter B. Fraser, a proponent of historical tourism, and opened as the "Oldest Wooden School House in the United States." The original coquina well and antiquated kitchen, filled with cooking utensils, are located within yards of the house.

Oldest Wooden School House Carrot Cake

Cake:
2 c flour
2 c sugar
3/4 t salt
2 t soda
2 t cinnamon, ground
4 eggs
1-1/2 c Crisco
3 c carrots, grated
1 c nuts, chopped

Frosting for cooled layer cake:
1 8 oz pkg cream cheese, softened
1 stick butter, softened
1 lb box confectioner's sugar
2 t vanilla
1-1/2 c nuts, chopped

Frosting for hot tube cake:
1 c sugar
1/2 t soda
1 c buttermilk
1 t cornstarch

Cake: Mix Crisco and sugar then add eggs one at a time. Sift in dry ingredients and mix well. By hand, mix in carrots and nuts. Pour into 3 layer pans or one tube pan greased and floured. Bake 30 minutes at 350° for pans, 1 hour and 15 minutes for tube.

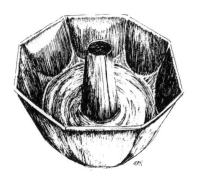

Allow to cool before icing. Yields 12-14 servings.

Frosting for cooled layer cake: Beat ingredients well. By hand, mix in nuts.

Frosting for hot tube cake: In saucepan bring to a boil all ingredients. Pour over hot cake in pan and let stand in pan for at least 24 hours. A chilled cake will be easier to slice.

Fraser Family Baked Beans

2 lg cans baked beans
1 lb bacon, fried, drained
1/2 c white sugar
1 c brown sugar
2 lg onions, diced
1/2 bell pepper, cored, diced
2 c ketchup
2 t Worchestershire sauce
1 8 oz jar Gulden's mustard

Combine all ingredients, mixing well. If mixture is too soupy add a bit more brown sugar. Pour into a casserole dish and bake 1 hour at 350°. Yields 8-10 servings.

World War II brought an end to historical preservation in St. Augustine. Once again military personnel headed to Florida for training with St. Augustine the destination for many. The government used local hotels, including the courtly Ponce de Leon, to house trainees. For the third time in less than a century, St. Augustine experienced an economic boom due to the presence of military personnel.

It was during the war years that Kenneth and Mary Dow painstakingly restored an eight-house historic estate which had last been owned as a group in the late 19th

century. The property to which they moved the dwellings was bounded by St. George, Bridge, and Cordova Streets. The Prince Murat House, on the corner of Bridge and St. George Streets, remained in its original position and was a part of the Dow's residence.

Murat House, c. 1790
Restored in the 1940s, late 1990s
at Old St. Augustine Village
250 St. George Street

The Murat cottage is one of the most distinctive structures in St. Augustine and has been used as a backdrop for various commercial advertisements. It was built of coquina in 1790 and later was named in honor of Prince Achille Murat, exiled nephew of Napoleon Bonaparte and son of the King of Naples who rented the house in 1824. In 1939, when Murat House was used as a restaurant, Greta Garbo was seen dining in a dark corner. In 1988, Kenneth Dow deeded this building and nine other historically rich St. Augustine buildings to the Museum of Arts and Sciences. The Murat House will be the site of an exhibit telling of the French in Florida.

Castle Warden, c. 1887
Remodeled in 1941 as
Castle Warden Hotel
Remodeled in 1951 as
Ripley's Believe It or Not!
19 San Marco Avenue

William Warden was a partner in the Standard Oil Company with John D. Rockefeller and Henry Flagler. Although Henry Flagler encouraged him to invest in St. Augustine, William Warden decided against the venture. Instead he vacationed in the city, building Castle Warden within view of old Fort Marion and the then-prominent San Marco Hotel. The winter residence originally had 19 bedrooms for him and his wife, their 14 children, and servants' quarters for five. William Warden imported Italian marble for the floors and installed a leaded glass skylight.

After the Wardens died one of their daughters lived in the house for a time and then sold it in 1941 to Norton Baskin and his wife, Marjorie Kinnan Rawlings, the noted author of the 1939 Pulitzer Prize winning novel, The Yearling. Norton Baskin had been an innkeeper in Ocala where he and Marjorie Kinnan Rawlings met when she lived at Cross Creek.

The Baskins remodeled the structure and renamed it Castle Warden Hotel. Norton Baskin ran the popular hotel and restaurant while Marjorie entertained prominent guests. In order to pursue her writing career, she often left Castle Warden, drove over the Bridge of Lions and down A1A to their Crescent Beach cottage or returned to her home at Cross Creek. In 1946 the Baskins sold the hotel to another innkeeper and moved to Crescent Beach.

Four years later, Robert Ripley's heirs purchased the property to display his extensive collection of oddities. Known as Ripley's Believe It or Not!, the tourist attraction opened in 1950 and became the prototype for later Ripley museums worldwide.

When the Armistice was declared at the end of World War II, the citizens of St. Augustine hurried to the Plaza to join in thanksgiving and celebration. They followed a tradition which started soon after the Plaza was established in 1598; during good times and bad, residents congregated together at the center of town.

The end of the war brought throngs of visitors to Florida. Additional motor courts, soon to be named "motels," appeared along US 1 and A1A. Tourist attractions were busy as life returned to its pleasant routines in the Ancient City: relaxation, entertainment, and hosting tourists.

C. F. Hamblen
General Store
c. 1875
The Oldest
Store Museum
c. 1962
4 Artillery Lane

Although there were 45 dry goods and general merchandise shops in St. Augustine by the late 1880s, the C. F. Hamblen General Store is the only one which remains in operation today. When C. F. Hamblen opened his store, a wide selection of items were sold including hardware, clothing, medicines, tobacco, household appliances, and groceries. The store was also the location for the neighborhood dentist, optometrist, blacksmith, gunsmith, and harness maker. When Henry

Flager began his building ventures in St. Augustine, his crews relied on supplies from Hamblens. In fact, if C. F. didn't have what the workmen needed, he would promptly order it. By 1908 Hamblen's was the third largest store of its kind in Florida.

Hamblen's Hardware is now located at 111 King Street. The earlier building at 4 Artillery Lane houses a collection of over 100,000 artifacts, most of which had been stored in the dusty attic warehouse. Now known as the Oldest Store Museum, it is an educational wonderland for viewing the extensive assortment of butcher tools, kitchen equipment, and antique food containers available to households during the 1800s.

Hotel Alcazar, 1889-1931
Remodeled in 1948 as
The Lightner Museum
75 King Street

The word Alcazar is Spanish for castle or fortress. Indeed, Henry Flagler's second hotel resembled one. The Hotel Alcazar closed its doors in 1931, a victim of the depression and the shift of wealthy tourists from St. Augustine to south Florida.

The building remained vacant until 1948 when Otto C. Lightner, founder of Hobbies Magazine, bought it to house his collection of over 20,000 hobbies, artifacts, and unique art objects. Two years later he bequeathed the museum and its contents to St. Augustine.

Today the city uses many of the former hotel rooms for government offices while the back portion of the building is the Lightner Museum. The ground floor contains numerous shops as well as a beautiful city commission boardroom.

The courtyard, where Otto C. Lightner is buried, also contains a stone bridge which spans a pool of colorful fish.

The Alcazar's former swimming pool, now emptied of water, is an eerie relic and reminder of a bygone age. Today it forms the centerpiece around which quaint antique shops and a cafe are situated.

Café Alcazar
Creamy Potato Vegetable Soup for a Crowd

1 lb butter
2 T salt
1 T pepper
5 large onions, roughly cut
5 lbs potatoes, roughly cut
3-5 broccoli or cauliflower heads
5 carrots, cut in large rounds
additional salt and pepper to taste

In a very large pot melt butter, salt and pepper. Add onions and saute until soft and then add potatoes. Cover with water. Add broccoli or cauliflower heads and carrots. Cover and cook on high, stirring occasionally. When potatoes are soft, remove pot from heat. Using ladle, transfer batches of vegetables with equal amounts of broth from pot to blender. Blend mixture until creamy consistency and place in a second very large pot. When all of vegetable and broth mixture have been blended, add ad-ditional salt and pepper to taste. Yields about 5 gallons or 80 one cup servings.

Café Alcazar
Curry Chicken Salad

16 small chicken breasts
4 ribs celery, finely chopped
1 c chopped parsley
1/2 c chopped green onion
1/2 c raisins
4 c mayonnaise
1/4 c honey
2 T curry
1/2 t salt
1/2 t pepper

Cook chicken, debone, and finely chop chicken breast meat. Combine with balance of ingredients and chill. Yields about 4 pints or 8 one cup servings.

Detail, Janie Young Price House

Africa, 1863
Renamed Lincolnville
in the 1880s
Start of Restoration early 1960s
South of Bridge Street

After President Lincoln's Emancipation Proclamation was read on January 1, 1863, many of St. Augustine's new Freedmen, eager to exercise their independence, moved to the west bank of Maria Sanchez Creek (presently Washington Street). There they built huts, rented land, tilled the soil, and named their small village Africa.

This new addition to St. Augustine was reached by a narrow wooden bridge which crossed Maria Sanchez Creek at the western foot of Bridge Street. At that time, the creek flowed half a mile further north, having once served as an ideal natural defense for the early Spanish settlers. With the establishment of Africa, the creek became a boundary of a different sort: a physical separation between blacks and whites in St. Augustine.

Less daring Freedmen remained at the homes of their former owners as house servants, nannies, or gardeners, living in cottages behind their place of employment. Due to the Emancipation Proclamation, they now were paid for their labor.

Africa's Best Chicken Pot Pie

4 chicken breasts, deboned, cooked, diced
1 stalk broccoli, thinly sliced
1/4 c carrots
1/4 c peas
1/4 c onions, diced
1/4 c mushrooms, thinly sliced
1 can cream of chicken soup, undiluted
2 c Bisquick
2 c chicken broth
1 c milk
1/4 c oil

Place chicken pieces in the bottom of a large baking dish. In a saucepan combine soup and broth and cook until smooth. Pour over chicken. Spread vegetables on top of mixture.

In separate bowl combine remaining ingredients and mix well. Pour over mixture in dish. Bake for 30 minutes at 400°. Yields 6-8 servings.

Since the Spanish occupation, blacks and whites in St. Augustine had been united in their efforts to defend the town when it was under attack and to survive during hard times. After the Civil War, the city's residents struggled to overcome physical and economic adversities left by the devastating conflict.

Although numerous former slaves relocated to the new village, their commitment to the St. Augustine community remained strong. Many blacks ran for public office and won. In 1873 William Van Dyke, a carpenter and butcher by trade, was elected the first black marshal of St. Augustine. He was followed in that position by another Black, Domingo M. Pappy. In 1882 Ed Houston, who had operated the ferry across the San Sebastian River after the Civil War, became St. Augustine's tax collector.

Another enterprising African American, Sonny Morals, filled his mule cart with flowers and vegetables to sell to the owners of the rapidly growing number of small hotels and boarding houses. Robert Welters opened Welters Restaurant on Charlotte Street near the Plaza.

Welters Creamy Cabbage

1 med cabbage, shredded
1 T onion, grated
1/4 c water
1 t salt
1/2 t pepper
1/2 c sour cream

In a saucepan combine all ingredients, except sour cream, cover, and simmer 5-10 minutes or until cabbage is tender. Stir in sour cream and heat. Yields 6 servings.

Peggy's Own Baked Beans

1 lg can baked beans
2 t mustard
1/2 - 3/4 c ketchup
3 T brown sugar
1 onion, halved
6 bacon strips

Combine all ingredients except onion and bacon strips and pour into a greased baking dish. Push onion down into mixture. Cover with bacon strips and bake at 350° until done, approximately 45 minutes. Yields 6-8 servings.

By the late 1870s and early 1880s a large portion of the residents in Africa were economically secure. They purchased land and built substantial homes, many of which are still standing. As the achievements of these former slaves became evident, concern arose among a small number of St. Augustine's whites who believed blacks were gaining too much political and economic influence. For this reason, a movement, though short-lived, was initiated to eliminate the Black vote for municipal elections.

Residents of Africa who had remained as tenant farmers after the Civil War, found it increasingly difficult to provide for their families. To supplement their needs, they sought employment as domestic help. The financial situation for most residents of St. Augustine, black and white, improved significantly when Henry Flagler moved to the city in 1885. He brought new building and rebuilding jobs to St. Augustine, as well as employment opportunities with his hotels and railway system.

Uncle Charley's Crescents

1/4 lb butter, softened
1/4 c powdered sugar
1-1/2 c flour
1/4 t lemon flavoring
1/2 t vanilla
1/2 c pecans, chopped
1/2 c powdered sugar

In large bowl mix all ingredients, except last item, by hand in order listed. Roll in crescent shape and bake 30 minutes at 300°. Remove from oven and sift remaining powdered sugar over all. Yields approximately 2 dozen.

Henry Flagler's decision to build a winter resort in St. Augustine had a startling and lasting impact on the city. The construction of the massive Hotel Ponce de Leon demanded hundreds of laborers. Black men left small farms and domestic *work to clear the land. They felled trees and pounded the trunks into the marshy soil to support the hotel structure. They filled in the northern portion of Maria Sanchez Creek, further isolating the village of Africa.*

The workers laid track so that Flagler's Railway could transport materials for the hotel's development and, ultimately, bring guests to the elegant resorts.

Lincolnville's Bar-Be-Que Ribs and Chops

Meat:
8 1" thick pork chops
3 lbs ribs
1/4 c oil
10 c water

Sauce:
2 c tomato sauce
1 c ketchup
2 T Worcestershire sauce
2 T hot sauce
1 T paprika
1 c brown sugar
1/2 c mustard
1/2 c onion, grated
1 T salt
1 T pepper
1/4 c vinegar

Sauce: Combine all ingredients.

Meat: Brown chops in skillet. Parboil ribs in water for 20 minutes. On large grill arrange meats and baste with sauce. Allow to cook several minutes then turn meat and baste. Continue basting and grilling for approximately 30 minutes or until meat is cooked through and is tender. Yields 12 servings.

Sometime during the 1880s, the residents of Africa changed the name of their community to Lincolnville to honor President Lincoln. They also worked for representation in government, employment with police and fire departments, and roadway construction throughout the community. By 1899 African Americans comprised one-third of St. Augustine's population, yet the influence they had held in local politics a decade earlier had eroded. By 1907 the first white primary was established and African Americans lost their right to vote in local elections.

Papa Clayton's Red Fish Stew

5 lbs catfish, deboned, cubed
1 lb fat back, cubed
8-10 med onions, chopped
3 cans tomato soup
3 soup cans of water
1 28 oz bottle of ketchup
2 lg cans whole tomatoes
1 oz bottle hot sauce
1/4 c Worchestershire sauce

In large pot fry fatback until brown. Remove meat and brown onions in grease. Add remaining ingredients, mix well, and simmer for 15 minutes. Add fish and cook on medium for 30 minutes. Turn off heat and let set for 2 hours. Yields 12 servings.

From the late 1800s through the 1940s, many of St. Augustine's African Americans prospered. In addition to working for Henry Flagler's expanding enterprises, they were successful entrepreneurs, skilled tradespeople, dock workers for the shrimping and fishing industries, hack drivers, and retail merchants in Lincolnville. Two of their businesses were Palace

Market, opened in 1914 by Frank Butler on Washington Street, and the Iceberg at 74 Bridge Street. The Iceberg, a soda fountain and drug store, was known citywide for serving the best ice cream in town.

By the 1950s, signs were posted in many parts of America proclaiming "whites only" or "colored only" at the entrances to restrooms or on drinking fountains. A few such signs appeared in St. Augustine as well.

Smithy's Ice Box Cookies

1 c Crisco
1 T salt
1 c brown sugar
1 c white sugar
2 eggs
1 c nuts, chopped
4 c flour
1/2 t soda
1 t cinnamon
1 t vanilla

Melt Crisco. Add salt and sugar. Add eggs one at a time then nuts and vanilla. Sift and measure flour. Add soda and cinnamon and sift again. Add to other mixture. Shape in rolls 2-1/2" in diameter and 8" long. Roll in wax paper and refrigerate over night. Next day slice and bake at 375° for 12 minutes. Yields approximately 2 dozen.

By the mid-1960s, racial discrimination had worsened in St. Augustine. Many businesses refused to serve the residents of Lincolnville. Unable to remain silent, St. Augustine's prominent African American leaders organized, joined by blacks and whites from Florida and beyond. The spring of 1964 ushered in marches to protest racial segregation.

The Southern Christian Leadership Conference sent its leaders to St. Augustine to assist: Dr. Martin Luther King, Dr. Ralph Abernathy, and Andrew Young. They stayed at the Lincolnville home of Janie Young Price on present-day Martin Luther King Avenue. During the marches, Henry and Kat Twine of Lincolnville joined Dr. King. Henry Twine became the first African American to serve as vice mayor. His wife, affectionately known as Miss Kat, was Lincolnville's matriarch.

Miss Kat's Sweet Potato Pie

Crust:
flour
Crisco
ice water
1 egg

Miss Kat's Hat worn during her march with Dr. King

Mixture:
sweet potatoes
2 sticks butter, softened
4 eggs
1 sm can Carnation evaporated milk
sugar
cinnamon, a good shake
nutmeg, a good shake
1 capful vanilla
pecans

Crust: Miss Kat says to make a pie crust you must use Crisco for the shortening and ice water to moisten. Add the flour and an egg and work it into a ball of dough. Roll out in a circle and place in a pie pan and prick the bottom with a fork. Cook in a 325° oven until slightly brown, perhaps 7 minutes. Set aside.

Mixture: While the pie crust is browning, boil some sweet potatoes until fork tender. Peel and mash with 2 sticks of softened butter. Add 4 eggs, Carnation evaporated milk, and sugar to taste. Add cinnamon, nutmeg, and vanilla. Mix thoroughly and pour into pie shell. Top with pecans and bake at 350° for 30 minutes or until knife blade comes out clean. Yields 6 servings.

Henry's Favorite Carrot Salad

6 lg carrots, scrubbed, sliced
1/4 c oil
1/4 c sugar
2 T vinegar
1 can tomato soup, undiluted
1 onion, chopped
1 bell pepper, cored, chopped
water

Cut some carrots in circles and steam in salt water until tender. Drain and set aside. Mix oil, sugar, vinegar, and soup. Heat on stove, stirring thoroughly. Add onion and bell pepper, then add carrots and mix together with sauce. Chill for several hours. Yields 4 servings.

St. Augustine's Civil Rights Marches became violent during the summer of 1964. Tempers flared, roadblocks were ordered, and the Ku Klux Klan demonstrated.

The events at the Plaza, the oldest public square in the United States, were captured by television cameras for all the world to see.

Lincolnville residents suffered economic hardships after those violent months of *1964. Even though the Civil Rights Act was signed into law on July 2, 1964, that summer signaled the decline of what had been a thriving African American community.*

Many Lincolnville residents lost their jobs; some relocated in search of employment while others remained. However, throughout Lincolnville's evolution, one characteristic remained constant; its residents were superlative cooks. Their ice cream parlors, bar-be-que stands, and restaurants offered delicious dishes with "a little of this and a little of that" creatively added to their foods.

Miss Judy's Mincemeat Cookies

3/4 c shortening
1-1/2 c sugar
3 eggs, well beaten
3 c flour
3/4 t salt
1 t soda
1 9 oz pkg mincemeat, finely crumbled
3 T water
1 c nuts, chopped

Cream shortening and sugar thoroughly. Add eggs and beat until light. Sift flour with salt and soda and add half to creamed mixture. Add mincemeat and water and stir until blended. Add nuts, then remaining flour. Mix well. Drop from a teaspoon on greased baking sheet and bake at 350° for 10-15 minutes. Yields approximately 2 dozen.

Culp's Famous Pecan Pie

1 9" pastry shell, uncooked
1/2 c sugar

1 c dark Karo syrup
4 T butter
3 eggs, well beaten
1 t vanilla
1 c pecans, chopped (may add more)

In saucepan melt together sugar, syrup, and butter. Remove from stove. In a bowl, mix together eggs, vanilla, and nuts. Slowly add the hot syrup mixture to the egg mixture. If you add it too fast the syrup will cook the eggs, so be careful. Pour into the pie shell and bake at 300° approximately 40-50 minutes or until filling is set at edges but slightly soft in the center. Yields 6 servings.

Grandmother's Christmas Sugar Cookies

My granddaughters and I had a good time cutting out Santas and Christmas trees and stars. We'd decorate them with red and green sugar and little candies. Grand-dad would sit at the kitchen table and watch. He didn't help, but he was good company. Those girls are grown now, but we have our memories and I'm glad they're keeping our tradition going. Life's good like that.

1/2 c shortening
1 c sugar
1 egg
3 c flour
1/4 t salt
3 t baking powder
1/2 c milk
1/2 t vanilla
red and green little sugar candies

Cream shortening and sugar thoroughly. Add egg and beat well. Sift dry ingredients (flour, salt, and baking powder) and add alternately with milk and vanilla. Mix thoroughly. Roll on lightly floured surface to 1/8" thickness. Cut with cookie cutter and decorate. Place on greased pan and bake at 350° about 15 minutes. Yields approximately 3 dozen.

New Year's Day Soul Food

Tradition has it that if you don't eat hog jowl, black-eyed peas, rice, and collards on New Year's Day, you won't have any money for the rest of the year.

Pea mixture:
1 hog jowl, teeth removed
1 lb black-eyed peas, soaked overnight
1 lg onion, chopped
1 t pepper
6 c water
3 c rice, cooked

Greens:
1 bunch collards
1 lg onion, chopped
1/2 lb salt pork or fresh ham
water

Pea mixture: Rinse peas in fresh water then place back in pot. Add remaining ingredients and simmer for 2-3 hours or until peas are tender. Serve over rice. Yields 6-8 servings.

Greens: Rinse greens several times to make sure all the grit is gone. Place in large kettle and add remaining ingredients. Cook down, about 1 hour. Serve with lots of cornbread and vinegar. Yields 4-6 servings.

Plaza de la Constitución

Chapter IX.
The Blending of Past and Present
1965 and Beyond

St. Augustine, Florida, the "Nation's Oldest Continually Occupied City," spent the better part of 1965 celebrating its 400th birthday. In honor of that momentous occasion, Florida's first outdoor drama, *Cross & Sword*, premiered in the city. The play told of St. Augustine's founding in 1565, portraying its hardships and its successes. For those who attended the play that year or the years that followed, they left the production with a sense of historical continuity and with the belief that St. Augustine was a survivor.

St. Augustine's 400th Birthday Cake

Banana cake:
1 box banana cake mix
2 lg bananas
1-1/4 c water
2 eggs
1/2 t almond extract

Topping:
8 med bananas, diced
1/2 c lemon juice
1-1/2 c sugar
1-1/2 t almond extract
1 pt whipping cream
1/2 c sugar
1 T vanilla flavoring

Cake: Combine mix, water, and eggs, and mix well. In a separate bowl mash bananas until mushy then add extract. Combine with mix and stir well. Pour into 2 8 x 9" cake pans lined with wax paper. Bake in a preheated 350° oven for 30-35 minutes. Remove from oven then cool 10 minutes.

Remove layers from pan and place on cooling racks. After the cake cools, split layers in half with thread.

Topping: While cake is cooking combine bananas, lemon juice, and 1-1/2 c sugar. Mix well. To this add vanilla extract and 1 t almond extract and mix gently. Cover and refrigerate. Prepare the following when the cake is ready to put together. To whipping cream add 1/2 c sugar and beat well. Then add 1/2 t almond extract.

Layer: Place bottom layer on cake plate cut inside up. Spread on 1/4 banana mixture on cake then cream. Place second half of cake cut side down. Layer 1/4 banana mixture then cream on cake. Place third layer on with cut side down. Spread mixture on cake then place last cake half cut side down. Spoon remaining mixture on top and sides. Yields 15-20 servings.

Although the mid-1960s ushered in the age of "instant foods" and TV dinners, St. Augustine's restaurants continued to thrive with their specially prepared seafood favorites. By the 1970s fast-food restaurants were haunted by those in a hurry, gaining in popularity as life became more frenetic. Evening meals around the family table and Sunday after church feasts began to disappear. Vegetarianism diets and health foods gained in popularity. The Space Age introduced freeze dried and dehydrated foods.

During this period, St. Augustine's reign as having one of the most prominent shrimping and fishing industries in the nation came to an end. However, nearby Hastings and Spuds continued exporting tons of baking and potato chip potatoes to northern markets.

Hotel Ponce de Leon
1888-1967
Remodeled in 1968
as
Flagler College
74 King Street

Two years after St. Augustine's 400th birthday, the magnificent, stately Hotel Ponce de Leon closed its doors. Motels had taken the place of grand hotels and tourist attractions farther south competed with old St. Augustine. The building, however, was in remarkably good shape. Eighty years earlier, when Flagler had been asked to justify the great sums of money he invested in constructing the hotel, he responded that:

> *I think it more likely I am spending an unnecessary amount of money in the foundation walls, but I comfort myself with the reflection that a hundred years hence, it will be all the same to me, and the building the better because of my extravagance.*
> *Henry Flagler, 1888*

Henry Flagler's reflection has proven to be correct. Over 100 years after its construction, the building stands largely unaffected by time. In 1968 it, as well as numerous structures surrounding the main building, became Flagler College. The College invested more than $30 million in the development and restoration of its unique campus. Private donations for restoration were also contributed by The Kenan Foundation, established by the family of Flagler's third wife, Mary Lily Kenan. The first electric hotel clock in the nation is still in operation in the elegant parlor where Flagler once entertained privately and where today's students and their parents often meet. Students and faculty congregate for meals in the grand dining room amidst antique furnishings from the hotel as light filters through the famous Tiffany stained-glass windows.

Flagler College
Sesame Spiced Chicken Soba

Meat and Pasta Mixture:
3 lb chicken breast, skinless, deboned
2/3 c vegetable oil
3 T garlic, minced
1 c celery, diagonally cut 1/4"
1/2 lb snow peas, cut lengthwise
1/2 lb bok choy, cut in thin strips
1 c tomatoes, chopped to 1/2"
4-1/2 lb Japanese Soba noodles, cooked
1/2 c peanuts, chopped

Marinade:
1 c sesame seed oil
1 c soy sauce
1/4 c cilantro, chopped
1/4 c green onions, chopped to 1/4"
3/4 c rice vinegar
1 T ginger root, peeled, grated
1/4 c sugar
1/2 t cayenne pepper, ground

Marinade: Combine ingredients and mix thoroughly. Place chicken in 3 c marinade, cover, and refrigerate for a minimum of 6 hours, maximum of 12 hours. Reserve remaining marinade for pasta.

Meat and Pasta: Preheat grill. Grill marinated chicken until internal tem-perature reaches 165° or until juices run clear. Julienne chicken into strips. Preheat wok or skillet. Add 1 T oil, swirl to coat surface. Add garlic, celery, peas, bok choy, and tomatoes. Stir fry until crisp-tender. Add remaining marinade, noodles, and chicken. Stir fry until heated through. Garnish with peanuts. Yields 12 servings.

Arroz Con Camarones

1 lb sm shrimp, peeled, deveined
2 c yellow or Spanish onions, chopped
   1/4"
1 c celery, chopped 1/2"
2 T garlic, minced
1 T whole fennel seed
2 c rice, uncooked converted
2-1/4 c water
2-1/4 c tomatoes, diced
1/4 c fresh parsley, chopped
2 T fresh mint leaves, chopped
1/2 t salt
1/2 t pepper
2 T olive oil

In brazier, sauté onion, celery, garlic, and fennel in olive oil until vegetables are tender. Add rice. Cook 2 minutes, stirring to coat rice with all. Add water, tomatoes, parsley, mint, salt, and pepper. Bring to a boil, reduce heat and cover. Simmer 30-40 minutes or until rice is tender. Add shrimp. Cook until shrimp turn pink. Yields 12 servings.

St. Augustine Light, 1874
Restored in 1992 as the
St. Augustine Lighthouse
Museum Complex
81 Lighthouse Avenue
Anastasia Island

After years of building wooden watch towers along the Atlantic Ocean, the Spanish constructed a durable coquina tower on Anastasia Island near the St. Augustine Inlet. When the British gained possession of La Florida, they extended the tower 60 feet in height by adding a wooden structure. A cannon was positioned atop the tower and fired to warn the fort of approaching ships.

By 1784 when Spain regained Florida, the city's engineer reported that the tower was still a "solid stone building, in the manner of an ancient Moorish castle, with ports and battlements," but that the wooden portion was in decay. The Spanish added a storehouse for powder and a kitchen. When La Florida was ceded to the United States in 1821, only the 44 foot high coquina tower was still intact, the wooden portion having been removed. The tower soon became a visitor attraction for St. Augustine's tourists.

Two years later, in 1823, the United States Congress appropriated $5,000 to convert the Spanish tower into a lighthouse. On April 3, 1824, Minorcan John Andreu, a harbor pilot, lit the lamp. As the years passed the height of the lighthouse was raised to 52 feet. In 1855 a fourth-order Fresnel lens replaced the earlier light. In 1859 the fifth lightkeeper, Joseph J. Andreu, fell to his death while whitewashing the tower. His wife, Maria, became the first female keeper of the St. Augustine Light. Her annual salary: $400. The following recipes are two favorites passed down from Maria's family.

Maria Andreu's Lettuce Salad

1 head butter lettuce
juice of 1 lemon
1/2 c black olives, sliced
1/4 c green olives, sliced
1 clove garlic, crushed
2 eggs, boiled, sliced
1/2 t salt
2 T olive oil
1 tomato, peeled, chopped
2 T red wine vinegar infused with
   datil peppers
1 t sugar
2 c water

Chop lettuce and immerse in water with lemon juice. In a separate container make dressing by combining garlic, salt, sugar, oil, vinegar, and mix well. Add tomato and olives. Drain lettuce then add dressing. Garnish with egg. Serve very cold. Yields 4 servings.

Joseph J. Andreu's Favorite Brown Bread

4 c flour, whole wheat
2 c flour, unbleached
4 T dry active yeast
2-1/2 c water, warm from tap
1/2 c white sugar
1-1/2 t salt
3 T olive oil
4 T butter

Dissolve yeast in water. Add sugar and unbleached flour and stir well. Let rest for 1-1/2 hours in a warm place. Dough will rise to almost double. Punch down then add salt, oil, and whole wheat flour. Lightly flour a board and knead dough about 325 times. Mold into an oval shape and let rise until double. Punch down and split into 2 loaves then knead each dough ball 20 to 30 times. Shape each loaf and place in a lightly greased bread pan. Allow to rise in a warm place until double in size. Bake at 325° for 35-45 minutes. If a soft top is desired, butter to prevent crusting. Yields 2 loaves.

By 1871 eroding shoreline had so endangered the Spanish coquina structure that Congress appropriated $60,000 to construct a new lighthouse. It was completed in 1873 as ocean waves swept within feet of the old light. On October 15, 1874, the new light was placed into service and the light atop the ancient sentinel was extinguished. Two years later the two-story lightkeepers' duplex was completed.

The lighthouse and the duplex are the oldest surviving brick buildings in St. Augustine. By 1880 the Spanish tower which, for a century, had guarded the coast, tumbled abruptly into a storm-tossed sea.

In 1918, Cardell Daniels, Sr., and his bride, Grace, moved to St. Augustine where Cardell had been appointed assistant keeper of the light. He served in that position for one year, returning in 1935 as the principal keeper of the light, remaining there until 1945. Two of the Daniels' five children tell happy stories about living at the base of the lighthouse.

As children, Wilma and her brother "Cracker" acted as tour guides when visitors wanted to climb the lighthouse. Tourists rode the tram across the wooden bridge from St. Augustine to Anastasia Island and the lighthouse. After the tourists descended the stairs, the children offered them a "free" postcard. Wilma and Cracker's gift often caused tourists to give them a nickel, a dime, or even a quarter. The children were thrilled with the money. Looking back on those carefree years Wilma remarked:

> *It cost a dime for the movies in town, and a nickel would buy a drink.*

Years later Wilma Daniels Thompson remembered wonderful meals her mother prepared in the lightkeeper's kitchen.

> The chickens were best because my Mom raised them herself, and she always had fresh eggs, too. I still have Mama's rolling pin and use it for good luck when I make this recipe!
>
> Wilma Daniels Thompson, 1998

Grace Daniels' Chicken and Dumplings

1 chicken, whole
scant cup of water
3 c flour
1 t salt
2 eggs
pepper to taste
water for boiling

In a large pot of water boil the chicken until done, approximately 1 hour. Remove from pot, cool, and debone. Make sure there are no bones left in the broth. Place the chicken aside and allow broth to simmer. Mix flour, eggs, water, salt, and pepper. Flour board and roll out dough using a floured rolling pin on a surface sprinkled with flour. Cut dough into long, narrow strips. Bring broth to boiling. Drop dough strips into boiling broth and cook until plump. Add chicken to broth and dumplings and let stew together for about 10 minutes. Yields 4 servings.

From 1926 to 1933 Alphonso C. Daniels was the second assistant lightkeeper. Rachel Daniels Lightsey, his daughter, reminisced over her teenage years at the St. Augustine Light and her mother Rebecca's Anastasia Island recipes.

Rebecca Daniels' Anastasia Island Lemon Coconut Cake

Cake:
1/2 lb butter
1-2/3 c sugar
2 c flour, plain
1 t lemon extract
5 eggs

Icing:
juice of 2 lemons
rind of 2 lemons, grated
2 eggs
1 c water
2 c sugar
1 T butter, melted
1 T cornstarch
1 c coconut, grated

Cake: Cream butter and sugar. Add eggs, then flour and extract. Beat well. Pour into 2 lightly greased and floured cake pans. Bake at 300° 45-55 minutes. Let cool.

Icing: In saucepan beat eggs and sugar. Add juice, rind, and butter, and mix well. Add water then cook until mixture starts to boil. Add cornstarch, stirring constantly. Remove from heat and add coconut. Let cool then spread between cake layers and on top. Yields 8-12 servings.

Lighthouse Loaf Cake

2 c butter
1 c sugar
2 eggs, beaten
1/2 c milk
1/2 t salt
1 t vanilla

2 c flour, leveled
2 t baking powder, level

Beat butter and sugar until light and creamy. Add eggs and stir. Then add milk and vanilla. Beat well. Add flour, salt, and baking powder. Mix together then pour into a greased and floured loaf cake pan. Bake at 350° for 45 minutes. Yields 12 servings.

In 1996 Rachel Daniels Lightsey was interviewed about growing up at the St. Augustine Light. She described the setting as it was during the first quarter of the 20th century.

On the Woods and the Beach: All around the lighthouse were woods. When we used to pick huckleberries early in the morning, we would take them and have them for breakfast down on the beach. We always cooked our breakfast down there.

On Tourists: Every day the keepers gave tours in the lighthouse starting at one o'clock. The horse and carriage used to bring the tourists to the lighthouse from town.

On Fishing: My daddy, of course, used to seine. Using seine nets, he pulled the fish into a big wash tub. I sold them to Corbett's Fish Market. (Corbett's was located near the Bridge of Lions on the mainland and across the street from the public market. During Rachel's childhood, the bridge to the island was wooden and Avenida Menéndez, which par-
continued on next column . . .

allels the Matanzas River, was called Bay Street.)

On the 1928 Hurricane (which lasted for three days): My mother was in the East Coast Hospital. You couldn't come to town. So I slept up there under the lens while my dad was on watch.

On Bird Island: We used to get one of the rowboats in the morning, before the sun came up and it was still dark, row over to Bird's Island (present day Conch Island in Anastasia State Park) . . . and the birds, thousands of nests and all kinds of seabirds, and we would pull the boat up and lay down and watch the sun come up. Then we'd cook our breakfast and then we'd swim until time to go back.

On the Garden: My dad had a garden back of where mother's kitchen was located. There was a large oak tree, a 100-year-old tree. They had a pump and that's where the ladies did laundry. (The Daniels' garden was not near the current lighthouse garden. It was on the other side of the house, closer to the street.)

We had trucks that came with fresh vegetables once or twice a week. Fruit and vegetables. Well, my daddy always had tomatoes and he loved to garden. There were collard greens and turnip greens in the wintertime. Beets. I remember beets that daddy cared for with a hoe and a
continued on next column . . .

rake. His little garden was fenced in so the animals didn't get in there from the woods.

On Barbecues: In front of the lighthouse (near where the present day Lighthouse Restaurant is located), we had barbecue pits, tables and chairs. People came from town and had dinners out there and weenie roasts and marshmallow roasts.

Oyster roasts, served with Worcestershire sauce, were a popular pastime for the lighthouse keepers, their families, and friends. Archaeological excavations on the lighthouse grounds uncovered bushels of discarded oyster shells as well as dozens of old glass-capped bottles which once contained Lea & Perrin's Worcestershire Sauce.

For all the years that the St. Augustine Light served those at sea, its keepers faithfully trudged 224 steps up and down the wrought-iron staircase, twice daily, to resupply the flame with lard oil, then later kerosene. The containers, when full, weighed as much as 50 pounds. Relief came for the keepers in 1936 when the lighthouse was electrified. The electrification of the light accelerated the revolution of the lens to every three minutes with a flash every 60 seconds.

The last keeper of the St. Augustine Light was James L. Pippin, who retired in 1955. By that time all of the lighthouse functions were automatically controlled so there was no longer a need for a keeper. With no one there to provide ongoing maintenance, the keeper's house fell into disrepair and later was damaged by fire.

In 1971 St. Johns County purchased the property. Continued vandalism spurred the Junior Service League of St. Augustine to undertake restoration of the lightkeeper's house. In 1981 the property was placed on the National Register of Historic Places. Following extensive restoration of the house and gardens, the complex was opened to the public in April 1992.

Today's visitors to the restored compound can step back in time to learn of those committed few who worked diligently to guard the sea and the shore. The beam transmitted by the first-order Fresnel lens atop the black and white striped tower sweeps across the horizon with a visibility of 19 nautical miles.

Florida East Coast Railway Building, 1924
Restored in 1996 as the
San Sebastian Winery
157 King Street

Winemaking in the New World had its origins in 1562 when the French Huguenots, led by Jean Ribault, established Fort Caroline, their ill-fated colony at the mouth of the St. Johns River. For their wines, the French picked the native wild scuppernong or muscadine grape which grew in abundance throughout the region. From the early days of San Agustín's beginnings as a military outpost, wine was a necessary commodity. Few people drank water as we do today; wines and ales were the choice of beverage and the native muscadine easily found favor with its full bodied, fruity taste. As late as 1886 the Genovar Market on Charlotte Street was manufacturing scuppernong wine.

Today, the native muscadine winemaking tradition continues in St. Augustine at the San Sebastian Winery.

Native Muscadine or Scuppernong Wine

8 c scuppernong grapes, perfect,
   washed thoroughly
white sugar
raisins

Place grapes in a large wooden or stone vessel. Mash them until all the skins are broken. Let grapes sit 24 hours. Using a cider press or other convenient kitchen equipment, express all the juice from the grapes. Measure juice then pour into a wooden keg or barrel. Discard skins and seeds. For every gallon of juice expressed add 2 pounds of sugar. Stir well. Cover the opening of the vessel with a piece of cloth so gas can escape and critters cannot enter. Allow to remain perfectly still in the barrel for 6 months. Remove liquid from barrel and pour into sterilized bottles, add-

ing 3 raisins to each bottle if desired. Cork bottles. Yields whatever amount of juice was strained from the grapes.

As one tourist wrote in the late 1800s:

> No one thought of rising early, and the first duty after breakfast was to lounge up St. George's Street to the Plaza.

For today's tourists, the local motels, inns, restaurants, and hotel continue to be conveniently located near the center of St. Augustine so that the old tradition of lounging up St. George's Street to the Plaza can remain a favorite pastime for visitors to the Ancient City. St. Augustine continues its tradition of entertaining and accommodating visitors. With one exception, motels have replaced Henry Flagler's sumptuous hotels. Unassuming boarding houses have evolved into quaint inns and notable restaurants now offer far more choices in foods and presentation than did the old corner cafes or diners.

Hotel Casa Monica
1888-1932
Restored in 1999 as the
Casa Monica Hotel
95 Cordova Street

The Hotel Casa Monica, a gracious hostelry, reflected St. Augustine's age of opulence until it was forced to close its doors in 1932, a victim of the Great Depression. Except for shops on the ground floor, it remained empty until 1962 when St. Johns County purchased the building for $250,000. The elaborate gardens at the rear of the building were asphalted over, the ornate balconies were removed, and

the regal bedrooms, parlors, and dining hall were remodeled for use as county offices.

In 1997 the county relocated its offices and a year later sold the building to a developer. In 1999 it was extensively restored and renamed the Casa Monica Hotel.

Casa Monica Rack of Lamb

6 French lamb racks
1 t rosemary
1/4 c Dijon mustard
1/4 c raspberry vinegar
1/4 c garlic, minced
1/8 c light brown sugar
1/4 c olive oil

Place all of the above ingredients, except lamb and olive oil, in a food processor or blender. With the machine running, slowly add the olive oil to form an emulsion. Spread approximately 2-1/2 T of the marinade on each lamb rack. Roast lamb in a preheated 400° oven until desired doneness, approximately 10 minutes

for medium rare. Garnish with extra marinade. Marinade will keep in the refrigerator for 3 weeks and is also good for pork, chicken, or beef. Yields 6 servings.

Chef Compton's Low Country Fried Grits

Grits:
2 c white hominy grits
1 c raw shrimp, diced
1/2 c scallions, diced
1/2 c sharp cheddar cheese, shredded
2 c chicken stock
1 c heavy cream
flour, salt, pepper for dredging
1/4 c butter

Bacon Gravy:
1 lb bacon, chopped
1 lg yellow onion, chopped
1 qt heavy cream
1 T creole spice
1/2 c flour
10 shrimp, grilled

Grits: Combine stock and cream in a large sauce pan and boil. Add grits and cook for 30 minutes over medium-high heat. Add shrimp, scallops, and cheese and simmer for 10 minutes. Pour mixture into a greased loaf pan and let chill overnight. The next day slice into 1/4" rectangles, dredge in flour seasoned with a pinch of salt and pepper, then pan-fry in butter until golden brown on each side.

Gravy: Cook bacon and onion over high heat until bacon is crisp. Do not drain grease. Add flour and blend well. Add cream and spice, stirring constantly until thick. Pour over fried grits and garnish each with a shrimp. Yields 10 servings.

Conch House Marina Resort
c. 1948
57 Comares Avenue
Anastasia Island

The Conch House was established by Jimmy Ponce, Sr. He and his family continue to operate the establishment which is located along the banks of Salt Run.

The Conch House Bar was designed to resemble the 1870s Capo Bath House which was located just north of the Plaza. It jutted into the Matanzas River so northern strangers could relax in the brackish tidal waters without having to travel to the ocean. A bathing schedule was established for the segregation of the sexes. Capo Bath House was used extensively until the great city fire of 1914.

Jackie's Baked Fish

6 oz fresh fish, filleted
1 oz parmesan cheese
3 oz sour cream
2 med onions, sliced
2 baking potatoes, peeled, sliced, steamed
2 tomatoes, sliced

Layer potato, onion, fish, and tomato. Spread sour cream on top and sprinkle with cheese. Bake at 350° for 15 minutes. Yields 2 servings.

Salt Run Shrimp and Artichoke Bake

2 artichokes, quartered
6 shrimp, shelled, diced
4 oz sour cream
4 oz mayonnaise
1 oz parmesan cheese
1/4 oz sherry
4 oz Monterey Jack cheese, grated

Mix sour cream, mayonnaise, parmesan, and sherry into a sauce. In well-greased baking dish, layer artichoke, shrimp, sauce, and top with Monterey Jack cheese. Bake at 350° for 10 minutes. Yields 2 servings.

Edward Masters House
c. 1883
Restored in 1984 as
Carriage Way Bed and Breakfast
70 Cuna Street

Edward Masters, a Minorcan, built this Victorian-style residence in the heart of the historic district adjacent to the former Spanish earthen Rosario Defense Line. In the 1940s the house was converted into an apartment complex and remained as such until 1984 when it was extensively restored and reopened as an inn.

Fritattas a la Carriage Way

10 eggs, beaten
1/2 c flour
1 t salt
1 t baking powder
1/2 c butter, melted
2 c cottage cheese
1 lb Monterey Jack cheese, grated
2 med zucchini, chopped
2 c mushrooms, sliced
1/4 c margarine
1 can mild green chili peppers, diced
1 c salsa, warmed

Combine first 7 ingredients. Sauté zucchini and mushrooms in marga-

rine and add to the egg mixture. Add peppers. Pour into a greased 9 x 13" baking dish and bake at 350° for 1 hour. Serve with salsa. Yields 4-6 servings.

Victorian Blueberry Stuffed French Toast

10 slices bakery-type bread, cubed
10 eggs, beaten
2 8 oz pkg cream cheese, cubed, softened
2 c milk
1-1/2 c blueberries, fresh or frozen
1 t vanilla
1/2 c maple syrup

In a 9 x 13" baking dish layer half of the bread, then all of the cheese, then all of the blueberries, then half of the bread. Combine all of the other ingredients and pour over layered mixture. Cover with plastic wrap and refrigerate overnight.

To cook cover with foil then bake in a 350° oven for 45 minutes. Uncover and bake 30 minutes more. Let set 25 minutes longer before serving. Yields 5-10 servings.

The Puller House, c. 1911
Restored in 1986 as
Casa de la Paz
22 Avenida Menéndez

This Mediterranean Revival style building was constructed for James D. and Minnie Puller. James Puller worked as an administrator for a small bank in St. Augustine, but within a few years became President of the First National Bank. The

Puller's home was built within the boundaries of the Spanish colonial city in the
section where the more prominent families were moving. Renamed Casa de la
Paz, it is located on Avenida Menéndez,
formerly Bay Street, overlooking the
Matanzas River.

St. Augustine has its ghost stories, one
of which involves the Puller House. Tradition has it that during the 1920s a
young woman visited the Pullers. While
there she suddenly took ill and died. Now,
every so often, the present owners are
awakened by the sensation of cold water
on the back of their neck. Music boxes in
the parlor play, yet when the owners walk
into the room to investigate, no one is
there.

House of Peace
Smoked Salmon Tarts

3 9" pie crusts, refrigerated
1-1/2 c half and half
4 eggs
1/4 lb smoked salmon, chopped
2 oz Monterey Jack cheese, shredded
1/4 c green onions, chopped
1/2 t dillweed, dried
1/4 t salt
1/4 t pepper

Preheat oven to 375°. Cut each pie
crust into 16 circles using a 2" biscuit
cutter. Place circles in greased miniature muffin cups. Mix half and half
with eggs in a large bowl using a
whisk. Stir in remaining ingredients.
Spoon 1 T filling into each shell. Bake
at 370° for 25 minutes or until golden
brown. Cool, remove from pans, and
store in a tightly covered container in
refrigerator. Yields 48 servings.

Bay View Chicken Salad
with Cranberry
Vinaigrette Dressing

Salad:
4 c chicken, cooked, diced
1 c celery, chopped
1/2 c mayonnaise
1/2 c sour cream
2 c grapes, white, seedless
1/2 t salt
1/2 t pepper
1/2 c pecans, toasted, salted, chopped

Vinaigrette:
3/4 c olive oil
1/4 c red wine vinegar
1 t salt
1 t sugar
1/2 t pepper
1/2 t paprika
1/4 t dry mustard
1/2 c cranberry sauce, whole

Salad: Combine ingredients well then
refrigerate.

Vinaigrette: In blender combine ingredients and blend until smooth. Refrigerate. At serving, pour over chicken
salad. Yields 8-10 servings.

Casa de la Paz

Carl Decher House
1893
Restored in 1990 as
Cedar House Inn
79 Cedar Street

Carl Decher, a carpenter and builder by trade, was enticed to St. Augustine during Henry Flagler's building boom era. Decker constructed this house just north of Lincolnville and convenient to the Hotel Alcazar. The orange groves and pecan orchards along Maria Sanchez Creek were perfect for an enthusiastic cook who only needed to exit the back door for fresh produce. Over the years, the house has had a variety of uses including a single family residence, a boarding house, and now a cozy, hospitable inn.

Cedar House Inn

Cedar House Inn's Ruffled Eggs

6 slices honey wheat bread
6 eggs
1 10 oz can cream of chicken soup
1/2 10 oz can yams or sweet potatoes, mashed
garlic powder
hot sauce
ground cinnamon
1 sm plum tomato, seeded, diced
1 T green onion, chopped
5 oz milk
non-stick spray
orange slices
strawberries
salt and pepper
paprika

Spray oil on bottom and sides of a "Texan" muffin tin. Press bread into bottom of tin to make bread shell. Have crust extend above top with a "ruffled" look. Break one egg into each shell and sprinkle with salt, pepper, and a dash of garlic. Bake at 350° for approximately 18 minutes or until eggs are just set. In a microwaveable pan, mix soup and milk. Stir in potatoes, a dash of hot sauce, and a dash of cinnamon. Microwave on high for 4 minutes. Top each egg with sauce, tomato, onion, and paprika. Garnish with orange and strawberry. Yields 3-6 servings.

Nina's Homemade Chocolate Chip Cookies

1/2 c white sugar
3/4 c margarine or Crisco, butter flavor
1/4 c dark sugar
1 egg
1/2 t salt
1 egg white
1 t baking soda
1-3/4 c flour

12 oz bag of chocolate chips
2 t vanilla

Cream together margarine and sugars. Blend in egg, salt, soda, and vanilla. Mix in flour then chocolate chips. Drop by rounded teaspoonful 2" apart on ungreased cookie sheet. Bake at 350° for 10 minutes. Yields approximately 18 cookies.

Castle Warden
Carriage House
c. 1887
Restored in 1990 as
Castle Garden
15 Shenandoah Street

First a carriage house, then a residence, and now an inn, Castle Garden was constructed from Anastasia Island's durable coquina stone and concrete. The stately Moorish-style building is adjacent to the original chimney from the old blacksmith shop.

Their Majesties' Spirulina Muffins

1 t spirulina
2 c oat bran cereal
1/2 c honey or molasses
2 t baking powder
1 c skim milk

Castle Garden

2 eggs, or whites only
2 T oil
1/2 t salt, optional

Heat oven to 425°. Line 12 medium muffin cups with paper cups or spray bottoms only with oil. Combine dry ingredients. Add milk, egg, honey, and oil, and mix until moistened. (For variation, fold in 1/2 c blueberries or 1 med mashed ripe banana, or 1/2 c raisins). Fill muffin cups almost full. Bake 15-17 minutes or until golden brown. Yields 12 servings.

Castle Garden Souffle

6 eggs
2 c milk
6 slices white bread
1 c cheddar cheese, grated
1 c meat, crumpled bacon, cut sausage
   links, or diced ham, cooked

Remove crust from bread and cut bread into cubes. Beat eggs and add milk, stir, then add cubes of bread. Let soak then beat with a mixer. Place in refrigerator overnight. Next morning pour 1/2 of egg mixture into the top of an oven-proof double boiler. Pour all the meat and 3/4 of the cheese over the mixture then pour the remaining egg mixture on top of that.

Sprinkle with additional cheese. Add water to the bottom of the double boiler. Place in the oven and bake for 1 hour or until golden brown. Yields 6 servings.

La Parisienne

La Parisienne, 1990
62 Hypolita Street

The French were thwarted in their efforts to establish a colony in La Florida when Menéndez, under orders from the King of Spain, descended on the French at their palisades fort near the mouth of the St. Johns River. He destroyed the fort, killed the settlers, and within weeks captured and executed the French leader, Jean Ribault, and 200 French Huguenot soldiers near San Agustín.

We salute the memory of these brave French pioneers by featuring a St. Augustine French restaurant. Although the building is relatively new, its architecture replicates the old coquina buildings of the Second Spanish Period.

Onion Soup Lyonnaise, Gratinee

1 gal chicken broth
1/4 c oil/butter blend
5 sweet onions (Vidalia) at room
  temperature, sliced with the grain
1/4 c flour
1/4 c port wine
1 oz cognac
1 loaf french bread, cut into 15 slices
1-1/4 lb gruyere cheese, grated
1-1/4 lb parmesan cheese, grated
parsley, chopped

Heat chicken broth. In heavy stock pot, heat oil on high. Add onions and brown well, stirring often. Add flour to make a roux. Cook 3 minutes and add hot chicken broth, port wine, and whisk. Bring to a simmer and cook for 1 hour. Add cognac and salt and pepper to taste. Place bread on baking sheet and sprinkle with cheese. Bake until cheese is partially melted. Place soup in bowls, top with bread, and place in heated oven until bubbly hot and cheese is melted. Sprinkle with parsley. Yields 15 servings.

Veal and Wild Mushrooms a la Ancient City

Veal chops:
8 10 oz veal chops (frenched veal rib)
flour
salt and pepper
1/4 c butter, clarified

Forestiere sauce:
1-1/2 lb mushrooms, domestic
1/2 lb mushrooms, crimini
1/2 lb mushrooms, porcini
1/2 lb portobello mushrooms or morels
1 lb leeks, white part, thinly sliced

1 c chicken broth
1/2 lb shallots, chopped
1/2 c cognac
1/2 c white wine
2 c beef broth
1 c cream

Veal chops: Cut chops in between bones, trim excess fat and season with salt and pepper. Heat a sauté pan. Dip chop in flour on one side only and brown in butter, flour side down. Cook until brown.

Sauce: In heated chicken broth soak mushrooms for 30 minutes. Remove, slice, and strain stock. Reduce stock, add to beef broth, and keep hot. Heat a stock pot and add butter then sauté leeks until wilted.

Add shallots, sauté 1 minute, add cognac, flame, add mushrooms, and wine. Cover pan and let "sweat" for 5 minutes. Add beef broth mixture and cream, reduce to correct consistency. Pour sauce over veal chops. Yields 8 servings.

Florida Cracker Cafe, 1990
81 St. George Street

A variety of definitions follow the Florida Cracker term for the country people who migrated to Florida after it became a United States Territory in 1821. No matter how or why the name originated, it describes hearty men and women whose tenacity in settling the backwoods of a primitive land secured their place in the state's history. Their special brand of cooking was a treat for northern "strangers."

Florida Cracker Cafe

Cracker's Best Key Lime Pie

Mixture:
3 cans Carnation sweetened condensed
   milk
8 egg yolks
6 oz Key West lime juice

Pie shell:
2 egg yolks
2 graham cracker pie crusts

Shells: Coat the crusts with egg yolks and bake at 375° for 5 minutes. Remove from oven and let cool.

Mixture: Mix milk and yolks in a mixer on medium speed. While still on medium, slowly mix in lime juice. After thoroughly blended, pour mixture into pie crusts and bake at 400° for 10 minutes. Remove from oven and let cool. Yields 2 pies.

Minorcan Clam Chowder for a Crowd

1 #10 can diced tomatoes
1 #10 can water
1 46 oz cans tomato juice
6 lbs potatoes, peeled,
   diced

Secret Garden Inn

1-1/2 lb carrots, peeled, diced
1/4 lb salt bacon
3-4 med onions, diced
3-4 med green bell peppers, cored, diced
1/4 c fresh thyme
1/2 c fresh basil
1-1/2 t datil pepper sauce
less than 1/8 c black pepper
1/3 c sugar
1/4 c clam juice
1 6 oz can tomato paste
5-6 bay leaves
1 51 oz can chopped clams, drained
1 51 oz can chopped clams, undrained

In a 5 gallon stock pot, add tomato juice, diced tomatoes, water, potatoes, carrots, clam base, and tomato paste. Heat on medium high heat. Sauté peppers and onions in salt bacon until transparent. Add all spices, peppers, and onions while stock is heating. Bring stock pot to a boil then reduce to medium heat and cook for approximately 45 minutes or until po

tatoes and carrots are tender. Add clams and clam juice. Heat for another 30 minutes while skimming froth from the top. Yields 3-1/2 to 4 gallons.

Marie Ward House, c. 1920
Restored in 1991 as the
Secret Garden Inn
56-1/2 Charlotte Street

This section of the Spanish colonial city was extensively damaged during two fires, one in 1887, then another in 1914. The house is located on one of the narrow streets that reflects the Spanish plans for laying out a town in the New World. It was built for use as a guest cottage and garage for the main house.

In the 1940s it became the Abernethy-Kitchens Typewriter Shop. From 1966 until 1979 it was the residence of Mrs. Harold Playter, the widow of a foreign service officer. Another owner, Marie Ward, was a professional singer who acquired the title "Songbird of the South."

Secret Garden's Cranberry Tea Bread

2 c all purpose flour
1-1/2 t baking powder
1/2 t baking soda
1/2 t salt
1 c sugar
1/2 c walnuts, finely chopped
2 c fresh cranberries, coarsely chopped
1 orange, grated rind and juice
1/4 c margarine, melted
1 egg, well beaten
water

Combine flour, baking powder, soda, salt, sugar, cranberries, and walnuts, and mix well. In separate bowl, combine rind, juice, margarine, and enough water to make 3/4 c mixture. Beat in egg. Pour over dry ingredients and mix just enough to dampen. Spoon into greased 9 x 5 x 3" loaf pan and bake in preheated 350° oven for 1 hour and 10 minutes or until done. Let sit 5-10 minutes, then turn out of pan and cool. Yields 10-12 servings.

Nancy's Pumpkin Soup

1 c canned pumpkin
2 t onion, finely chopped
1/4 t curry powder
1 can chicken broth (10-1/2 oz)
3/4 t salt
1 c half and half
parsley, finely chopped for garnish
2 T butter

Cook onion and curry powder with butter until onion is soft but not brown. Stir, then cover and simmer approximately 10 minutes. Remove from heat and combine with pumpkin, chicken broth, and salt in a blender. Blend until smooth. Return to pot, add cream, and heat slowly. Serve with a sprinkling of parsley. Yields 2-3 servings.

Thomas Adams House, c. 1900 Restored in 1995 as Bay Breeze Cottage
4 Tremerton Street

The property on which this Victorian house is located was granted by the Spanish Crown to José Ximenez in 1793. When La Florida became a United States Territory in 1821, the land passed to Joseph Smith of Charleston, South Carolina. It lies just south of the colonial Rosario Defense Line and near the site of the early 18th century Seminole Indian village of La Punta.

Bay Breeze Cottage is a two and a half story Victorian vernacular structure. From 1904 to 1912 the house was the residence of Thomas Adams, deputy collector of customs and later assistant manager of the Ancient City Wagon Works which repaired the carriages owned by the St. Augustine Transfer Company. The original stone cistern, used to capture rain water for drinking and bathing, is adjacent to the house.

La Punta Crabmeat Cobbler

Cobbler:
3 c crabmeat
3 c tomatoes, crushed
1/2 c olive oil
1 c sharp cheese, grated
1/2 c green peppers, cored, chopped
1/2 c onions, chopped
1/2 c plain flour, sifted

Bay Breeze Cottage

1 c dry mustard
2 t rum
1 c milk
1/2 t salt

Topping:
1 c plain flour
1/4 c sharp cheese, shredded
2 T baking powder
2 T shortening
1/2 c milk
1 t salt

Cobbler: Combine oil, pepper, and onions and simmer until tender, about 10 minutes. Blend in flour, mustard, milk, and cheese. Stir constantly until cheese is melted and mixture is very thick. Add crabmeat, tomatoes, rum, and salt. Blend thoroughly. Pour into a greased 2 qt casserole dish. Bake 30 minutes at 325°.

Topping: Sift flour, baking powder, and salt into a mixing bowl. Add cheese. Cut in the shortening thoroughly un-til the particles are fine. Add milk and mix only until all the flour is moistened. Drop rounded teaspoonsful on top of hot crabmeat mixture. Bake at 400° until biscuits are browned. Yields 8 servings.

Bay Breeze Cooler

This recipe, minus the rum, of course, dates back to the 1940s when orange groves along well traveled Highway 41 to south Florida advertised free juice for tired tourists.

3 scoops orange sherbet
1 jigger orange juice, freshly squeezed
1 jigger rum (optional)
1 jigger ginger ale
3 ice cubes
1 orange, thinly sliced

Combine all ingredients in a blender and blend until frothy. Pour into wine glass garnished with half an orange slice. Yields 2 servings.

Conclusion

St. Augustine began as a Spanish military outpost in 1565, became a haven for the sick in the 19th century, and today is one of the most popular tourist destinations in the United States. It has endured wars and depression, bleak winters and raging hurricanes; even pirates and prejudice.

Known for years as the "The Oldest City," St. Augustine is much more. We who live here also consider it to be "The Hospitable City," filled with remarkable people who have welcomed strangers to their doors for centuries. The reason for St. Augustine's success as a vacation spot was predicted as early as the 1820s when Dr. Andrew Anderson's first wife, Mary, wrote of her new town:

> *The very Demon of leisure presides in this Renounced City. The nature of the climate is too congenial to all kinds of rest both body and mind.*

Nature and history have always befriended St. Augustine. It is no different today. Our beautiful natural surroundings have been enriched by the diversity of previous cultures: Native Americans, Hispanics, British, Africans, and others. Tourists have also added to this vibrancy. Through the years, people have come and people have gone. Buildings have been razed or restored. Yet one constant has remained: St. Augustinians have always managed to create a congenial environment for their visitors.

We hope that *Flavors of St. Augustine* has served you well as an historical cookbook of our Nation's Oldest City. We also hope that it has given you a deeper appreciation for our city of five flags and a thousand flavors.

Index

_Other books in this series
include: America's First
City, St. Augustine's His-
toric Neighborhoods; An
Uncommon Guide to
Florida; Henry Flagler,
Visionary of the Gilded
Age; and for younger
readers Henry Flagler,
Builder of Florida._ Con-
tact your bookseller or
Tailored Tours Publica-
tions, Box 22861, Lake
Buena Vista, FL 32830 at
1-800-354-5246.